LIFE AND TEACHING *of the* MASTERS OF THE FAR EAST

VOLUME 1

by

Baird T. Spalding

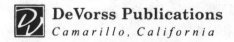

DeVorss Publications
Camarillo, California

Life and Teaching of the Masters of the Far East, Volume 1
Copyright © 1924, 1937 by Baird T. Spalding
Revised Edition Copyright renewed, 1964
ISBN10: 0875163637
ISBN13: 9780875163635

Life and Teaching of the Masters of the Far East, 6-Volume Set
ISBN10: 0875165389
ISBN13: 9780875165387

DeVorss & Company, Publisher
P.O. Box 1389
Camarillo CA 93011-1389
www.devorss.com

Printed in the United States of America

THE LIFE AND TEACHING

OF THE

MASTERS OF THE FAR EAST

By BAIRD T. SPALDING

Baird T. Spalding, whose name became legend in metaphysical and truth circles during the first half of the 20th century, played an important part in introducing to the Western world the knowledge that there are Masters, or Elder Brothers, who are assisting and guiding the destiny of mankind. The countless numbers of letters that have come in through the years, from all over the world, bear testimony of the tremendous help received from the message in these books.

Partial listing of the contents of the six volumes:

VOLUME 1: Introduction of the Master Emil ~ Embarking from Potal, India with Jast and Neprow ~ Visiting the "Temple of Silence" ~ Astral Projection ~ Walking on Water ~ The Healing Temple ~ Emil talks about America ~ The Snowmen of the Himalayas ~ New Light on the teachings of Jesus. ISBN 9780875163635

VOLUME 2: Visit to the Temple of the Great Tau Cross ~ Visit with the Master Jesus ~ The Mystery of thought vibrations ~ Jesus feeds the multitude ~ A healing experience ~ Jesus and Buddha visit the group. ISBN 9780875163642

VOLUME 3: A Master speaks of the Christ consciousness ~ The nature of cosmic energy ~ The creation of the planets and the worlds ~ The trip to Lhasa ~ Visiting the Temple Pora-tat-sanga ~ Explaining the mystery of levitation ~ A doubter becomes convinced of the existence of Jesus. ISBN 9780875163659

VOLUME 4: This material was first presented as "The India Tour Lessons." Each chapter has text for study, as well as guides to teachers for developing and interpreting the material. Among subjects covered: The One Mind ~ Basis of Coming Social Reorganization ~ Consciousness ~ Prana. ISBN 9780875163666

VOLUME 5: Material taken from lectures given by Mr. Spalding in California during the last two years of his life ~ A brief biographical sketch ~ Camera of past events ~ Is there a God? ~ The Divine Pattern ~ The Reality ~ Mastery Over Death ~ The Law of Supply. ISBN 9780875163673

VOLUME 6: 18 articles by Mr. Spalding, with questions & answers, taken from *Mind Magazine,* 1935-1937 ~ A contemporary biographical sketch ~ Special section includes rare photos of Spalding, the India Tour group, shipboard accommodations, Calcutta ~ Rare letters from the tour and other Spalding memorabilia ~ Seven manuscripts by Spalding include: Original of the Lord's Prayer; Divine Mastery; Eternal Youth; Rising Out of Limitation; The Power of Thought ~ Spalding Eulogy and personal insights. ISBN 9780875166988

BOXED SET VOLUMES 1-6: ISBN 9780875165387

PUBLISHER'S NOTE

Both Mr. Spalding and Mr. DeVorss (who knew Mr. Spalding personally) died in the 1950's. The people who were associated with Mr. Spalding on the tour have also passed on. We are therefore without contact with anyone who has firsthand knowledge of the work, and the books themselves are now the only source of information. To our knowledge, there is no map available of the tour, and we know of no photographs. We have tried at various times to locate additional records, as well as camera information, but without success. We sincerely regret that we have no additional information to offer.

DEVORSS & COMPANY

FOREWORD

IN PRESENTING *The Life and Teaching of the Masters of the Far East* I wish to state that I was one of a research party of eleven persons that visited the Far East in 1894.

During our stay—three and a half years—we contacted the Great Masters of the Himalayas, who aided us in the translation of the records, which was of great assistance in our research work. They permitted us to enter into their lives intimately and we were thus able to see the actual working of the great Law as demonstrated by them. We call them Masters, which is merely our name for them. One living the life described herein is entitled to reverence and consideration as a Master.

Records and manuscripts—our actual experience with the Masters—were preserved. Personally, at that time, I thought the world was not ready for this message. I was an independent member of the research party and I am now publishing my notes under the title *Life and Teaching of the Masters of the Far East*, with the thought that the reader may accept or reject, as he wishes.

This book, which will be followed by others of the Sun series, gives the first year's experience of the expedition in relation to the Masters. It includes their teaching, which was taken by us stenographically at the time, with their permission and approved by them.

The Masters accept that Buddha represents the Way to Enlightenment, but they clearly set forth that Christ IS Enlightenment, or a state of consciousness for which we are all seeking—the Christ light of every individual; therefore, the light of every child that is born into the world.

(Signed) Baird T. Spalding

CHAPTER I

THERE is so much being printed at the present time regarding spiritual matters, and there is such a great awakening and seeking for the truth regarding the great teachers of the world, that I am prompted to place before you my experience with the Masters of the Far East.

In this book I am not attempting to expound upon a new cult or religion; I am only giving a resume of our experience with the Masters, in which I am undertaking to show the great fundamental truths of their teaching.

These Masters are scattered over a wide territory and, since our metaphysical research covered a large portion of India, Tibet, China, and Persia, no attempt to authenticate these experiences is made.

There were eleven practical, scientifically trained men in our party. The greater part of our lives had been spent in research work. We had been accustomed to accept nothing unless it was fully verified and we never took anything for granted. We went thoroughly skeptical and came away thoroughly convinced and converted, so much so that three of our number went back determined to stay until they are able to perform the works and live the life, just as these Masters are living today.

Those who so greatly assisted us in our work requested that their names be withheld in the event of our publishing the expedition's memoirs. I shall relate nothing but the facts as they happened, using, as nearly as possible, the words and expressions of the people I met and with whom I was thrown in daily contact during the expedition.

It was one of the conditions of the agreement before taking up the work that we should at first accept as fact everything we witnessed, and no explanations should be demanded until we had gone into the work thoroughly, taken their lessons, lived and observed their daily lives. We were to accompany these Masters, live their lives, and determine for ourselves. We were at liberty to be with them as much as we liked, ask any questions we wished, use our own deductions in getting results, and finally accept what we saw as fact or fake. There was no effort at any time to influence our judgment in any way. They wished us to become thoroughly convinced before we gave credence to anything we saw or heard. Therefore, I will place these happenings before the readers and ask them to accept or reject as they see fit.

We had been in India about two years, doing regular routine research work, when I met the Master known in these writings as Emil. While walking along a street in the city where we were staying, my attention was attracted to a crowd. I saw the center of interest was one of the street magicians, or fakirs, that are so common in that country. As I stood there I noticed beside me an elderly man who was not of the same caste as those about him. He looked at me and asked if I had been long in India. I replied, "About two years." He asked, "Are you English?" I answered, "American."

I was surprised and very much interested to find one who spoke English. I asked him what he thought of the performance then going on. He answered, "Oh, it is a common occurrence in India. These fellows are called fakirs, magicians, and hypnotists. They are all the name implies; but underneath it all is a deeper spiritual meaning that few discern, and good will come of it some day. It is but the shadow of the thing from which it sprang. It has caused a great deal of comment, and those commenting upon it seem never to have reached the true meaning, for there certainly is a truth underneath it all."

Here we parted and I saw him only occasionally during the next four months. Our expedition was confronted by a problem which gave us a great deal of trouble. In the midst of our worries I again met Emil. Immediately he asked what was bothering me and began talking about our problem.

I wondered at this, for I felt that none of our party had mentioned it outside of our little circle. His familiarity with the situation was such that I felt the whole matter was known to him. He explained that he had a certain insight into the affair and that he would endeavor to help.

Within a day or two the matter was cleared up, leaving us without a problem. We wondered at this but, with other things to occupy our time, soon forgot.

As other problems came up it became a habit with me to talk them over with Emil. It seemed that as soon as I discussed our troubles with him they would cease to exist.

My associates had met and talked with Emil but I had said little to them about him. By this time I had read a number of books on Hindu lore, selected by Emil, and I was fully convinced that he was one of the adepts. My curiosity was keenly aroused and I was becoming more deeply interested each day.

One Sunday afternoon Emil and I were walking in a field when he called my attention to a pigeon circling overhead and casually remarked that the bird was looking for him. He stood perfectly still and in a few moments the bird alighted upon his outstretched arm. He said the bird has a message from his brother in the North. This proved to be a fellow-worker who had not reached the attainment whereby he could communicate directly, so he took this means. We later found that the Masters are able to communicate with each other instantly by thought transference or, as they call it, a force much more subtle than either electricity or wireless.

I then began to ask questions and Emil showed me that he was able to call the birds to him and direct their flight while they were in the air; that the flowers and trees would nod to him; that the wild animals would come to him fearlessly. He parted two jackals that were fighting over the body of a smaller animal that they had killed and were feeding upon. When he approached them they stopped fighting and put their heads in his outstretched hands in perfect trust, then resumed their meal in quiet. He even gave me one of the young wild creatures to hold in my hands. He then said to me, "This is not the mortal self, the self you see, that is able to do these things. It is a truer, deeper self. It is what you know as God, God within me, God the Omnipotent One working through me, that does these things. Of myself, the mortal self, I can do nothing. It is only when I get rid of the outer entirely and let the actual, the I AM, speak and work and let the great Love of God come forth that I can do these things that you have seen. When you let the Love of God pour through you to all things, nothing fears you and no harm can befall you."

Every day during this time I had lessons with Emil. He would suddenly appear in my room, even if I had taken special care to lock the door before retiring. At first his appearance at will disturbed me but I soon saw that he took it for granted that I understood. I became accustomed to his ways and left my door open so that he could come and go as he pleased. This confidence seemed to please him. I could not understand all his teachings and I could not accept them fully, nor was I able, with all I saw while in the East, to fully accept at the time. It required years of meditation to bring me the realization of the deep spiritual meaning of these peoples' lives.

Their work is accomplished without ostentation and in perfect childlike simplicity. They know the power of love to protect them and they cultivate it until all nature is in love with them and befriends them. Thousands of the common people are killed annually by serpents and wild animals, yet these Masters have so brought forth the power of love in themselves that serpents and wild animals do not injure them. They live at times in the wildest jungles, and sometimes lay their bodies down before a village to protect it from the ravages of wild animals, and no harm befalls the village or themselves. When occasion requires they walk on water, go through fire, travel in the invisible, and do many other things that we have been accustomed to look upon as miracles performed only by one supposed in some way to possess supernatural powers.

There is a striking resemblance between the life and teaching of Jesus of Nazareth and those of these Masters as exemplified in their daily life. It has been thought impossible for man to derive his daily supply directly from the Universal, to overcome death and to perform the various so-called miracles that Jesus performed while on earth. The Masters prove that all these are their daily life. They supply everything needed for their daily wants directly from the Universal, including food, clothing and money. They have so far overcome death that many of them now living are over five hundred years of age, as was conclusively proved by their records.

There are comparatively few of these Masters in India, other cults seeming to be but offshoots of their teaching. They realize their number is limited and that only a few scholars can come to them. In the invisible, however, they can reach almost unlimited numbers and it seems to be the greater work of their lives to reach out into the invisible and help all who are receptive to their teaching.

The teaching of Emil laid the foundation for the work which we were to take up years later in our third expedition to these countries, during which time we lived with the Masters continuously for three and one-half years, traveled with them, and observed their daily lives and work throughout the Far East.

CHAPTER II

FOR the outset of our third expedition, in which we took up the metaphysical research work, our little party assembled at Potal, a small village in the remote part of India. I had written Emil that we were coming but did not write the object of the trip nor did I even mention the number in our party. Much to our surprise we found complete preparations had been made for our entire party and that Emil and his associates knew our complete plans. Emil had rendered us a remarkable service while in Southern India but the service rendered from this time on surpassed all description. To him and the wonderful souls we met I wish to give all credit for the success of the entire undertaking.

We arrived at Potal, from where the expedition was to start, late in the afternoon of December 22, 1894, and found we were to start Christmas morning upon what was to be the most memorable expedition of our whole lives. I never shall forget the few words Emil said to us that morning. These words were delivered in fluent English, although the speaker did not boast an English education, and he had never been out of the Far East.

He began by saying, "'Tis Christmas Morning; to you I suppose it is the day Jesus of Nazareth, the Christ, was born; to you the thought must come that He was sent to remit sins; to you He must typify the Great Mediator between you and your God. You seem to appeal to Jesus as a mediator between you and your God, who seems to be a stern and, at times, an angry God sitting off somewhere in the place called heaven, located where I do not know, except it be in man's consciousness. You seem to be able to reach God only through His less austere and more loving Son, the great and noble One whom we all call Blessed and whose advent into the world this day commemorates. To us this day means more; to us this day not only means the advent into this world of Jesus, the Christ, but also this birth typifies the birth of Christ in every human consciousness. This Christmas Day means the birth of the Great Master and Teacher, the Great Liberator of mankind from material bondage and limitations. To us this great soul came on earth to show more fully the way to the real God, the great Omnipotent, Omnipresent, Omniscient One; to show that God is all Goodness, all Wisdom, all Truth, All in All. This Great Master, who came to this world this day, was sent to show more fully that God not only dwells without us but within us, that He never is, nor can be, separated from us or any of His creations; that He is always a just and loving God; that He is all things; knows all things; knows all and is all Truth. Had I the understanding of all men, it is beyond my power to express to you, even in an humble way, what this Holy Birth means to us.

"We are fully convinced and we hope you also will see that this Great Master and Teacher came to us that we might have a fuller understanding of life here on earth; that all mortal limitations are but man-made and in no other way should they be interpreted. We know that this greatest of all teachers came to show more fully that the Christ in Him and through whom He did His mighty works is the same Christ that lives in you, in me, and in all mankind; that we can, by applying His teachings, do all the works that He did and greater works. We believe that Jesus came to show more fully that God is the one great and only Cause of all things, that God is All.

"You may have heard it said that we believe Jesus received his early training among us. Perhaps some of us do believe. Let that be as it is. Does it matter whether His training came from among us or as a direct revelation from God, the one source where all things really exist? For when an idea from God-mind has been contacted by one man and sent out through the spoken word, cannot one, or all, again contact that thought in the Universal? Because one has contacted the idea and sent it out, it does not follow that it is his particular possession. If he did appropriate and hold it, where would be room for receiving? To receive more we must give out what we have received. If we withhold what we receive, stagnation will follow and we will be like the wheel that generates power from the water and suddenly, of its own volition, begins to withhold the water which it is using. It will soon find itself stifled with inert water. It is only when the water is allowed to flow freely through that it is of value to the wheel to create power. Just so with man. When he contacts God's ideas he must give them out in order to receive the benefit from them. He must allow all to do the same, that they may grow and develop as he is growing.

"I am of the opinion that what Jesus taught came to Him as a direct revelation from God, as it no doubt has come to our great teachers. Are not all things of God, and whatever one human being can do, cannot all do? We believe you will be convinced that God is ever willing and ready to reveal Himself to all men as He has revealed Himself to Jesus and others. The only requisite necessary is for each one to be willing to let God come forth. We believe, with all sincerity, that all are created equal; that all men are

[17]

one man; that the mighty works done by Jesus can and will be done by all. You will see there is nothing mysterious about these works. The mystery is only in man's mortal concept of them.

"We fully realize you have come to us with minds more or less skeptical. We trust you will live with us and know us as we really are. Our work and the results accomplished, we leave you to accept or reject, as you will."

CHAPTER III

WE LEFT this village for Asmah, a smaller one, about ninety miles distant. Emil assigned two younger men to accompany us. These men — fine, erect specimens of the Hindu type — were to have charge of the entire expedition. The perfect ease and poise with which they accomplished their task, surpassed any of our former experiences. For convenience of identification, I am calling these two men Jast and Neprow. Emil was the one that received us and looked after our welfare at the village from which we took our departure. He had had many more years' experience than the others. Jast was the executive head of the expedition, while Neprow was his assistant and saw that all orders were carried out.

Emil sent us away with a few remarks, in which he said, "You are about to start on your expedition with these two men, Jast and Neprow, to accompany you. As you travel it will take about five days to journey to your next important stopping place, about ninety miles distant. I will tarry here for a time because it will not be necessary for me to consume that time to cover the distance, but I will be there to greet you. I wish to ask that you leave one of your party here, in order to make observations and corroborate what may happen. In this way, time will be saved and he will be able to join the expedition not later than ten days hence. We simply ask him to watch and report what he sees."

We started with Jast and Neprow in charge of the expedition and I wish to say that more business-like arrangements could not well be imagined. Every detail was complete and swung into line with the rhythm and precision of music. This harmony was maintained throughout the entire expedition, which lasted three and half years.

I wish here to add my impressions of Jast and Neprow. Jast was a fine upstanding Hindu—kind, efficient, with no bluff or bluster. Every order he gave was almost in a monotone and executed with precision and snap that caused us to wonder. From the very outset we could see a fineness of character that caused much comment. Neprow, a wonderful character, was here, there and everywhere, always cool, collected and a marvel of efficiency. There was always the same calm, accompanied by quiet precision of movement, with wonderful power to think and execute. This was so marked that every member of the expedition commented upon it. Our Chief remarked, "Those fellows are wonderful. It is a relief to find people who can think and execute."

We arrived at the appointed village about four o'clock of the fifth day and there was Emil to greet us, as he had agreed. Can you imagine our amazement? We were quite certain we had come by the only traveled route and by the swiftest mode of locomotion in that country, except as the couriers go. They travel in relays and go night and day. Here was a man well advanced in years, as we thought, and one we felt would in nowise be able to negotiate a journey of ninety miles in less time than it required us to do the same—yet, here he was.

Of course we all tried to ask questions at once and were eager to hear. These were his words, "I said when you departed that I would be here to greet you—I am here. I wish to call your attention more fully to the fact that man in his right domain is limitless, knows no limit of time or space. Man, when he knows himself, is not obliged to toil wearily along for five days to accomplish ninety miles. Man in his right estate can accomplish any distance, it matters not the magnitude, instantly. A moment ago I was in the village from which you departed five days ago. What you saw as my body still reposes there. Your associate, whom you left in that village, will tell you that, until a few moments before four o'clock, I conversed with him, stating that I would go to greet you as you would arrive here about this hour. What you saw as my body is still there and your associate still beholds it, although it is at present inactive. This was done simply to show you that we are able to leave our bodies and greet you at any appointed place, at any specified time. The two who accompanied you could have accomplished the journey as I have. In this way you will more readily realize that we are only ordinary humans of the same source as you; that there is no mystery but that we have developed the powers given all by the Father, the Great Omnipotent One, more fully than you have. My body will remain where it is until night, then I will bring it here and your associate will proceed on his way here as you did, arriving in due time. After a day's rest we will journey to a small village, one day off, where we will tarry one night, then return here and meet your associate to see what his report will be. We will assemble this evening in the lodge. In the meantime, farewell."

In the evening, after we had assembled, Emil, without opening the door, suddenly appeared in our midst and said, "You have seen me appear in this room, as you would say, by magic. Let me say there is no magic about it. Here is a simple experiment which you can behold. You can see this, consequently you will believe. Kindly gather around so that you can see. We have a small glass of water which one of your number has just brought from the spring. You see that a minute particle of ice is forming in the very center of the water. You see it gather to itself, particle by particle, more ice, until now the whole of the water in the glass is frozen. What has happened? I held the central atoms of the water in the Universal until they became formed or, in other words, I lowered their vibrations until they became ice and all the other particles formed around them until the whole has become ice. You can apply this to the little glass, the tub, the pond, the lake, the sea, the whole mass of the water of the earth. What would happen? All would be frozen, would it not? To what purpose? None. You ask by what authority. I say by using a perfect law. But in this case, to what end? Nothing, as no good has been accomplished or could be accomplished. Had I gone on determined to carry this out fully, what would have happened? The reaction. To whom? To me. I know the law and what I express returns to me as truly as I express it. Therefore, I express only the good and the good returns to me only as good. You can readily see that, had I persisted in the freezing, the cold would have reacted upon me long before I had accomplished the end and I would, in reaping the harvest of my desire, have been frozen. Whereas, if I express the good, I reap the harvest of my good eternally.

"My appearance in this room tonight may be explained in this way. In the little room where you left me I held my body in the Universal by raising its vibrations and it returned to the Universal or, as we say, returning it to the Universal where all substance exists. Then, through my I AM, my Christ Consciousness, I held my body in my mind until its vibrations were lowered and it took form right here in this room and you could see it. Wherein is there any mystery? Am I not using the power, or the law, given me by the Father through the Beloved Son? Is not this Son you and I and all mankind? Wherein lies the mystery? There is none.

"Consider the faith represented by the mustard seed. It comes to us from the Universal through the Christ within, which has already been born within us all. As a minute speck it enters through the Christ, or superconscious mind, the place of receptivity within ourselves. Then it must be carried to the mount or highest within ourselves, the very top of the head. It is held there. We must then allow the Holy Spirit to descend. Now comes the admonition, 'Thou shalt love the Lord, thy God, with all thy heart, with all thy soul, with all thy strength and with all thy mind.' Think! Does the meaning come? Heart, Soul, Strength, Mind. Is there anything to do at this point but to turn it all over to God, the Holy Spirit, the Whole-I-Spirit in action? This Holy Spirit comes in many ways, perhaps as tiny entities tapping and seeking admittance. We must accept and allow this Holy Spirit to come in and unite with the minute point of light or seed of knowing and revolve around it and adhere to it just as you saw the particles of ice adhere to the central particle, and it will grow in form particle by particle, circle by circle, just as the ice, multiply and express that seed of knowing until you are able to say to the mountain of difficulties, 'Be thou removed and cast into the sea,' and it will be done. Call this fourth dimension or what you wish, we call it God in expression, through the Christ in us.

"It is in this way the Christ was born. Mary, the Great Mother, perceived the ideal; the ideal was held in mind, then conceived in the soil of her soul, held for a time there, then brought forth or born as the perfect Christ Child, the First Born, the Only Begotten, the Son of God. He was nourished and protected; given the very best of the mother; watched over and cherished until He grew from childhood into manhood. It is thus the Christ comes to all of us;

first as an ideal planted in the soil of our soul—the central part where God is—held in mind as the perfect ideal, then brought forth or born as the perfect Child, the Christ Consciousness.

"You who have seen what has been accomplished here doubt your own eyes. I do not blame you. I get the thought of hypnotism from the minds of some. My brothers, is there one here who feels that he does not have the power to exercise every Godgiven faculty that he has seen brought forth tonight? Do you think for a moment that I am in any way controlling your thought or vision? Do you think that I could, if I would, cast a hypnotic spell over any or all of you—for did you not all see? Is it not recorded in your own great Book that Jesus entered a room with the doors closed? He just came in as I have done. Do you think for a moment that Jesus, the Great Master and Teacher, needed in any way to hypnotize? He used His own God-given power as I have done tonight. Let me say that I have done nothing but what each one of you can do. Not only you, but every child that is or has been born into this world, or universe, has the same power to do just what you have seen accomplished this night. I wish to get this clearly before your minds. Let me also say that you are individuals, that you are not personalities, that you are free wills, not automatons. Jesus did not need to hypnotize and we do not need to hypnotize. Doubt us all you wish until you are fully satisfied as to our honesty. Put the idea of hypnotism away for the time, or at least let it lie passive until you have gone deeper into the work. All we ask is that you keep an open mind."

CHAPTER IV

A S THE next stage of our journey was to be in the nature of a side trip, we left the main part of our outfit and the next morning proceeded on our way to a small village about twenty miles distant, with only Jast accompanying us. The trail was not of the best and at times was very difficult to follow as it wound through the dense forests peculiar to that country. We arrived at our destination just before sunset that evening, tired and hungry, as we had pushed on all day with only a short noonday halt for lunch. The country in general was rough and uneven and the trail seemed practically unused. It was necessary to cut our way through occasional thickets of trailing vines. At each delay Jast seemed impatient. We wondered at this for he had previously seemed so poised. This was the first and only time during the three and a half years he was with us that he was not the same cool, collected Jast that started with us. Later we did not wonder at his unrest in the light of what transpired.

We entered the little village of about two hundred inhabitants one-half hour before sunset and, when it was known that Jast was with us, I believe every villager, old and young, and every pet and domestic animal came to greet us. While we were the object of more or less curiosity, it was immediately noted that Jast was the center of interest, greeted by all with the utmost reverence. After a few moments he said a word to the villagers and all but a few returned to their usual duties. Jast turned to us and asked if we wished to go with him while the camp was being prepared for the night. Five of our party said they were tired after the day's journey and wished to rest.

The remainder of us followed Jast and the handful of villagers toward the far side of the clearing that surrounded the village. After crossing the clearing we had gone but a short distance into the jungle when we came upon the form of a man lying upon the ground as though dead — that was our impression at first glance. A second glance, however, showed that the repose suggested calm sleep rather than death.

We stood staring as though transfixed for we saw that the figure lying on the ground was Jast. Suddenly, as Jast walked toward it, the figure became animated and rose to a standing position. As the figure and Jast stood face to face for an instant, there was no mistaking the identity — it was Jast. All saw that it was he. Then, instantly, the Jast we had known had disappeared and there was but one figure standing before us. Of course, all this was accomplished in much less time than it takes to tell and the wonder was that not one of us questioned. The five who had been left behind at camp came running without a signal from any of us. We afterwards asked them why they came. The answers were, "We don't know. The first we knew, we were all on our feet and running to you. We simply do not know why we did it. None of us recall any signal. We found ourselves running in your direction before any of us realized what we were doing."

One of our number remarked, "My eyes are opened so wide that I see far beyond the vale of death and the wonders that stand revealed are beyond conception." Another said, "I see the whole world overcoming death. How vividly the words come back, 'The last enemy, Death, shall be overcome.' Is not this the fulfillment of these words? What pigmies are our mere intellects in comparison with this gigantic but simple understanding and yet we have dared to look upon ourselves as giants of intellect. Why, we are mere babes! I just begin to see the meaning of, 'Ye must be born again.' How true the words!"

I leave the reader to imagine our surprise or bewilderment. Here was a man with whom we had been in daily contact, and by whom we had been served daily, that was able to lay his body down for the protection of others and go on and serve so very efficiently. Could it do otherwise than recall, "He that is greatest among you, shall be servant or shall serve." I think there was not one among us but from that moment lost all fear of death.

These people are accustomed to laying a body down before a village in the jungle of a country infested with marauding men and animals and that village is as safe from the ravages of men and animals as though it were in a civilized country.

It was very evident that Jast's body had been lying where we found it for a considerable time. The hair had grown long and bushy and in it were the nests of a little bird peculiar to the country. These birds had built their nests, reared their young, and the young had flown away, thus giving unmistakable evidence of the time the body had been in that position and inactive. These birds are very timid and will abandon their nests at the slightest disturbance. This shows the great love and trust of the little birds.

The excitement was so great that no one in our camp, except Jast, slept that night. He slept like a child. At intervals one or another of our party would sit up and look over toward where Jast was sleeping, then lie down again, saying, "Pinch me to see if I am really awake." Occasionally a more forceful expression was used.

CHAPTER V

WE WERE up at sunrise the next morning and that day returned to the village where we had left our outfit. We arrived at the village just before dark and pitched our camp under a great banyan tree. The next morning Emil greeted us and we all began asking questions. He said, "I do not wonder at your questions and I will gladly answer all that I can at this time, leaving others until you have gone further into our work. In talking to you as I am, you fully realize that I am using your language to convey to you the one great underlying principle of our belief.

"When all know the Truth and it is rightly interpreted, truly is it not one and all from the same source? Are we not all one with the universal mind substance, God? Are we not all one great family? Is not every child, everyone born, no matter the caste or creed, a member of this great family?

"You ask if we believe death is avoidable. Let me answer in the words of the Siddha: 'The human body is built up from the individual cell, like the bodies of plants and animals, whom we love to call younger and less evolved brothers. The individual cell is a minute microscopic unit of the body. By a process of growth and division, repeated many times, this minute nucleus of a cell-unit results at last in a complete human being, built up of almost countless millions of cells. These body cells specialize for certain different functions but they retain, in the main, the characteristics of the individual cell whence they arose. This individual cell may be looked upon as the torch bearer of animate life. It passes on from generation to generation the latent fires of God — the vitality of all living beings, with an unbroken ancestry reaching back to the time when life first appeared on this planet.' This individual cell has the property of unlimited youth. But what about the group cells called the body? The group cells arose from the individual cell repeated many times, retaining its individual characteristics, one of which is the latent fire of life, or Eternal Youth. The group cells, or body, function as guardian of the individual cell only during the short span of life as you know it now.

"The most ancient of our teachers by inspirational means perceived the truth of the fundamental unity of life reactions in plant and animal. We can well imagine these teachers beneath the spreading banyan addressing their pupils as follows: 'Look at this giant tree. The vital process going on in our brother, this tree, and in ourselves is fundamentally the same. Behold the leaves and the buds at the tips of the oldest banyan — how young they are — young as the seed from which the giant sprang into life. The life reactions of plant and man being alike, man can certainly profit by the experience of the plant. As the leaves and buds at the tips of the branches of the oldest banyan are as young as the seed whence it sprang, even so the group cells in man forming his body, need not gradually lose their vitality and die, but may grow young and evergreen as the ovum or individual cell itself. Indeed, there is no reason why your body should not grow as young and vital as the vital seed from which it sprang. The ever-spreading banyan, always a symbol of everlasting life, does not die except through accident. No natural law of decay, no old age process seems to exist within the banyan tree to affect injuriously the vital energy of its cells. The same is true of the human form divine.

"There is no natural law of death or decay for

man, except through accident. No inevitable old age process exists within his body or group cells — nothing that can gradually paralyze the individual. Death is, then, an avoidable accident. Disease is, above all, dis-ease, absence of ease or Santi — sweet, joyous peace of the spirit reflected through the mind in the body. Senile decay, which is the common experience of man, is but an expression that covers his ignorance of cause, certain disease conditions of mind and body. Even accidents are preventable by appropriate mental attitude. Says the Siddha: 'The tone of the body may be so preserved that it may naturally resist with ease infectious and other disease, like plague and influenza.' The Siddha may swallow germs and never develop disease at all.

"Remember that youth is God's seed of love planted in the human form divine. Indeed, youth is the divinity within man; youth is the life spiritual — the life beautiful. It is only life that lives and loves — the one life eternal. Age is unspiritual, mortal, ugly, unreal. Fear thoughts, pain thoughts, and grief thoughts create the ugliness called old age. Joyous thoughts, love thoughts, and ideal thoughts create the beauty called youth. Age is but a shell within which lies the gem of reality — the jewel of youth.

"Practice acquiring the consciousness of childhood. Visualize the Divine Child within. Before falling asleep suggest to your consciousness, 'I now realize that there is within me a spiritual joy-body ever young, ever beautiful. I have beautiful, spiritual mind, eyes, nose, mouth, skin — the body of the Divine Infant, which now, tonight, is perfect.' Repeat this affirmation and meditate upon it quietly while falling asleep. Upon rising in the morning suggest to yourself aloud, 'Well, dear (addressing yourself by name), there is a divine alchemist within.' By the spiritual power of these affirmations during the night a transmutation takes place and the unfolding from within, the Spirit, has saturated this spiritual body and spiritual temple. The inner alchemist has caused dead and worn-out cells to fall and the gold of new skin to appear with perpetual health and loveliness. Truly divine Love in demonstration is eternal youth. The divine alchemist is within my temple, constantly coining new and beautiful baby cells. The spirit of youth is within my temple — this human form divine, and all is well. Om Santi! Santi! Santi! (Peace! Peace! Peace!)

"Learn to smile in the sweet way of a child. A smile from the soul is spiritual relaxation. A real smile is a thing of true beauty, the artistic work of the 'Inner Ruler Immortal.' It is well to affirm — 'I think a kind thought for all the world. May all the world be happy and blest.' Affirm before taking up the work for the day — 'Within me there is a perfect form — the form Divine. I am now all that I desire to be! I visualize daily my beautiful being until I breathe it into expression! I am a Divine Child, all my needs are being now and forever supplied!'"

"Learn to thrill yourself. Affirm, 'Infinite Love fills my mind and thrills my body with its perfect life.' Make everything bright and beautiful about you. Cultivate a spirit of humor. Enjoy the sunshine.

"You understand that I am quoting from the teaching of Siddha. They are the oldest teachers known and their teaching antedates all history by thousands of years. They went about teaching the people and showing them the better way of life even before man knew the simple arts of civilization. It is from their teaching that the system of rulers sprang. But these rulers soon wandered away from the realization that it was God expressing through them. Thinking it was themselves, the personal, who were doing the work, they lost sight of the spiritual and brought forth the personal or material, forgetting that all comes from the one source—God. These rulers' personal concepts gave rise to the great separations in belief and the wide diversity of thought. This is our concept of the Tower of Babel. The Siddha have preserved throughout the ages the true inspirational methods of God expressing through mankind and through all His creations, realizing that God is All and that it is God manifesting through all. They have never deviated from this teaching. Thus they have preserved the great fundamental Truth."

CHAPTER VI

A S WE had considerable work to do before crossing the Himalayas, we decided upon this village as the most opportune place for our headquarters. The man we had left in the village to observe Emil joined us here and reported that he had conversed with Emil until nearly four o'clock of the day he was to keep his appointment with us. Then Emil said he was about to keep his appointment. His body immediately became inactive and reposed upon the couch as though asleep. It was in this position until about seven o'clock in the evening, when it gradually became more indistinct and disappeared. It was at this time in the evening that Emil came to us in the lodge at the little village.

The season was not far enough advanced for us to attempt the mountain passes. You will note that I say, for us. By this I mean the members of our little party, for by this time we had begun to look upon ourselves as mere impediments. We realized that our three great friends — you will note that I call them all great, for indeed they were — could have negotiated the distance that we covered in far less time than it took us but they were uncomplaining.

We had made a number of short trips from our headquarters with either Jast or Neprow accompanying us and in every instance, they had shown their sterling qualities and worth. On one of these trips Emil, Jast, and Neprow accompanied us to a village where a temple called The Silence Temple, The Temple Not Made By Hands, is located. This village contains the temple and the houses of the attendants and is located on the former site of a village that had been nearly destroyed by the ravages of wild animals and pestilence. We were told that the Masters visited this spot and found a few inhabitants left of about three thousand population. They ministered to them and the ravages of the wild animals and pestilence ceased. The few villagers vowed that, if they were spared, they would, from that time on, devote their lives to God, serving Him in any way He chose. The Masters left and when they returned later they found the temple erected and attendants in charge.

The temple is very beautiful, situated on an elevation overlooking a wide expanse of country. It is about six thousand years old, is made of white marble, and has never needed repairs, as a piece chipped off replaces itself, as was proven by members of our party.

Emil said, "This is called the Temple of Silence, the Place of Power. Silence is power, for when we reach the place of silence in mind, we have reached the place of power — the place where all is one, the one power — God. 'Be still and know that I am God.' Diffused power is noise. Concentrated power is silence. When, through concentration (drawing to a center), we have brought all of our forces into one point of force, we have contacted God in silence, we are one with Him and hence one with all power. This is the heritage of man. 'I and the Father are one.' There is but one way to be one with the power of God and that is consciously to contact God. This cannot be done in the without, for God manifests from within. 'The Lord is in His holy temple; let all the earth keep silent before Him.' Only as we turn from the without to the silence of the within can we hope to make conscious union with God. We will realize that His power is for us to use and we will use it at all times. Then we will know that we are one with His power.

"Then will humanity be understood. Man will learn to let go of self-delusions and vanities. He will realize his ignorance and littleness. Then will he be prepared to learn. He will realize that the proud cannot be taught. He will know that only the humble can perceive the Truth. His feet will feel the firm rock, he will no longer stumble, he will be poised in decision.

"To realize that God is the only power, substance, and intelligence may be confusing at first. But when man does realize the true nature of God and brings Him forth into active expression, he will use this power at all times. He will know that he consciously contacts His power at all times — when he eats, when he runs, when he breathes, or when he does the great work before him. Man has not learned to do the greater works of God because he has not realized the greatness of God's power and has not known that God's power is for man's use.

"God does not hear us through our loud and vain repetitions nor our much speaking. We must seek God through the Christ within, the invisible connection which we have within ourselves. When the Father within is worshiped in Spirit and Truth, He hears the calls of that soul which sincerely opens to Him. The one who makes the connection with the Father in secret will feel the power flowing through him as the fulfillment of every desire. For he that sees the Father in the secret place of his own soul and there abides, him the father will reward openly. How often Jesus disclosed his individual contact with the Father. See how He constantly held Himself in conscious communication with God within. See how He talked with Him as though He were personally present. See how powerful this secret inner relation made Him. He recognized that God does not speak in the fire, the earthquake, or the great wind, but in the still, small voice—the still, small voice deep in our own souls.

"When man learns this, he will become poised. He will learn to think things through. Old ideas will drop away, new ideas will be adjusted. He will soon find the ease and efficiency of system. He will learn at last to take all the questions that perplex him into this silent hour. There he may not solve them but he will become familiar with them. Then he will not need to go hurrying and battling through the day and feel that his purpose has been defeated.

"If man would come to know the greater stranger —himself—let him enter his own closet and shut the door. There he will find his most dangerous enemy and there will he learn to master him. He will find his true self. There will he find his truest friend, his wisest teacher, his safest adviser—himself. There will he find the altar upon which God is the undying fire, the source of all goodness, all strength, all power— himself. He will know that God is in the deepest part of the silence. He will find that within himself abides the Holy of Holies. He will feel and know that his every desire is in God's mind and is, therefore, God's desire. He will feel and know the closeness of the relationship of God and man, the Father and the Son. He will realize that only in consciousness has there been any separation of these which have seemed two—just as his spirit and his body have seemed to be two—but which in reality are one.

"God fills both heaven and earth. It was this great revelation that came to Jacob in the silence. He had slept on the stone of materiality. In a great burst of divine illumination he saw the outer is but the out-pressing or expression of the image held within. So impressed was he by this that he called out, 'Surely the Lord (or law) is in this place (the earth or body) and I knew it not. This is none other but the house of

God and this is the gate to heaven.' Man will realize, as Jacob did, that the real gate to heaven is through his own consciousness.

"It is this 'ladder' of consciousness, revealed in a vision to Jacob, which each of us must climb before we can enter that silent secret place of the Most High and find that we are in the very center of every created thing, one with all things visible and invisible, in and of the Omnipresence. In Jacob's vision he was shown the ladder reaching from earth to heaven. He saw the angels of God descending and ascending upon it — God's ideas descending from Spirit to form and ascending again. It was the same revelation that came to Jesus when the 'heavens were opened unto him' and he saw the wonderful law of expression whereby ideas conceived in the divine Mind come forth into expression and manifest as form. So perfectly was this law of expression revealed to the Master that at once he saw all form may be transformed, or changed in form, through a change of consciousness in regard to it. His first temptation was to change the form of stones to that of bread to satisfy personal hunger, but with the revelation of this law of expression came the true understanding that stones as well as all other visible forms have come forth from the Universal Mind Substance, God, and are in themselves true expressions of divine Mind; and all things desired, (not formed) are still in this Universal Mind Substance ready to be created or brought forth to fill every desire. Thus, the need for bread but showed that the substance with which to create bread or any other needed thing is at hand without limitation and bread can be created from this substance just as well as stones can be created therefrom. Every good desire man has is God's desire; therefore, there is an unlimited supply in the Universal God Substance all about us to fill every desire. All we need do is to learn to use what God has already created for us and this He wills to have us do that we may be free from every limitation and thus be 'abundantly free.'

"When Jesus said, 'I am the door,' He meant that the I AM in each soul is the door through which the life, power, and substance of the great I AM, which is God, comes forth into expression through the individual. This I AM has but one mode of expression and that is through idea, thought, word, and act. This I AM God Being, which is power, substance, intelligence, is given form by consciousness; and for this reason the Master said, 'According to your faith be it unto you,' and 'All things are possible to them that believe.'

"Now we see that God is within the soul as power, substance, and intelligence — or in spiritual terms, wisdom, love and truth — and is brought out into form or expression through consciousness. The consciousness which is in the infinite mind of God and in man is determined by the concept or belief that is held in mind. It is the belief in separation from Spirit that has caused our forms to age and die. When we see that Spirit is all and that form is constantly being expressed from Spirit, then shall we understand that that which is born of or brought out of Spirit is Spirit.

"The next great truth to be revealed through this consciousness is that each individual, being a concept of the divine Mind, is held in that mind as a perfect idea. Not one of us has to conceive himself. We have been perfectly conceived and are always held in the perfect mind of God as perfect beings. By having this realization brought to our consciousness, we can contact the divine Mind and so re-conceive what God has already conceived for us. This is what Jesus called being 'born again.' It is the great gift the silence has to offer us; for by contacting the God-mind we can think with God-mind and know ourselves as we are in reality rather than as we have thought ourselves to be. We contact God-mind through true thought and so bring forth a true expression; whereas, in the past, perhaps through untrue thought, we have brought forth an untrue expression. But, whether the form be perfect or imperfect, the Being of the form is perfect God-power, substance, and intelligence. It is not the Being of the form that we wish to change but the form that Being has assumed. This is to be done through the renewing of the mind, or through the change from the imperfect to the perfect concept, from the thought of man to the thought of God. How important then to find God, to contact Him, to be One with Him and to bring Him forth into expression. How equally important is the silence or the stilling of the personal mind, that the God-mind in all its splendor may illumine the consciousness. When it does, then we shall understand how 'the sun of righteousness (right-use-ness) shall rise with healing in his wings.' The mind of God floods consciousness as sunshine floods a darkened room. The infusion of the Universal Mind into the personal mind is like the entrance of the vastness of the outside air into the impurity of that which has long been held in some close compartment. It stands alone, supreme, and we realize that we are to build but one temple. The Temple of the Living God is the blending of the greater with the lesser through which the lesser becomes one with the greater. The impurity was caused by the separation of the lesser from the greater. The purity is caused by their union, so that no longer is there a greater and a lesser but just the one good, whole, pure air. Even so must we know that God is One and all things visible and invisible are One with Him. It is separation from Him that has caused sin, sickness, poverty, and death. It is union with Him that causes one to become a whole Being or to become conscious of being whole.

"The separation from unity is the descent of the angels on the ladder of consciousness. The return to unity is the ascent of the angels upon the ladder. The descent is good, for unity then becomes expressed in diversity, but in diversity there need be no concept of separation. That which is diversity has been misconceived from the personal, or external viewpoint, to be separation. The great work for each soul is to lift the personal viewpoint to such heights in consciousness that it becomes one with the whole. When all can 'meet with one accord in one place,' that place in consciousness where it is understood that all things visible and invisible have their origin in the one God, then we stand upon the Mount of Transfiguration. At first we see Jesus and with Him Moses and Elias; or Law and Prophecy, and the Christ, (the power within man to know God); and we think to build three temples, but the deeper meaning comes. We are given to realize the immortality of man and to know that divinity is never lost, that Divine man is deathless, eternal. Then Moses—the Law, and Elias—the Prophecy, disappear; and the Christ stands alone supreme and we realize that we have to build but one temple—the Temple of the Living God within our very selves. Then the Holy Spirit fills the consciousness and the sense delusions of sin, sickness, poverty, and death become no more. This is the great purpose of the silence.

"This temple from which you may chip a piece and the scar will be instantly healed but typifies the temple of our body, of which Jesus spoke, the temple not made by hands, eternal in the heavens, which we are to bring forth here on earth."

CHAPTER VII

W E RETURNED from our trip and found a number of strangers gathered at the village. They were gathering from the country about and a number of the Masters were congregating for a pilgrimage to a village about two hundred and twenty-five miles distant. We wondered at this for we had been in that direction and found that the trail traversed what we called a sandy desert. It was in reality a high plateau covered with sandhills that the wind had shifted back and forth and where but little vegetation grew. Beyond this desert the trail led over a small range of mountains which is a spur of the Himalayas. That evening we were invited to accompany the expedition and were told we would not need to take the more cumbersome part of our outfit, as we would return before crossing the main Himalayas. The expedition was to start the following Monday.

Of course Jast and Neprow had everything in readiness and early Monday morning we swung into line with about three hundred others. The greater portion of these had infirmities for which they were seeking healing. All went well until the following Saturday, when there arose the most severe thunderstorm we had ever experienced. There was a perfect downpour for three days and nights, a forerunner of summer, as they called it. We were camped in a very convenient place and did not suffer from the storm. Our greatest anxiety was about provisions for we were certain that this prolonged delay would cause serious inconveniences to all concerned, as there was but enough brought along for the trip, not counting delays. This delay seemed doubly serious to us for, as we saw it, there was no place to replenish our supplies unless we returned to our starting point, possibly one hundred and twenty miles distant, a greater portion of which lay over the sandy desert already referred to.

Thursday morning the sun rose clear and beautiful but, instead of pushing on as we had expected, we were told that we would wait where we were until the trails had dried and the rivers had receded so we could proceed more comfortably. We were all fearful lest our provisions should be exhausted and one of our party voiced this fear. Emil, who had charge of the whole outfit, came to us and said, "You need not fear. Does not God take care of all His creatures, both great and small, and are we not His creatures? You will see that here I have a few kernels of corn or corn seed. I will plant them. By this act I have definitely said that I want corn. I have formed corn in my mind. I have fulfilled the law and in due season it will come forth. Is it necessary for us to await the long, arduous process that Nature in her slow growth and unfoldment will take in order to grow corn? If so, we would be obliged to wait a long, hard time to obtain it. Why not use a higher or more perfect law, given us by the Father, to produce it? All that is required is to become quiet and visualize or idealize corn and we have corn cured, ready for use. If you doubt it, you can gather it, grind it into meal, then make it into bread." There before us was corn grown and cured so that we did gather it, and grind it, and afterwards made it into bread.

Then Emil went on to say, "This you have seen and believe but why not use a more perfect law and bring forth a more perfect thing or exactly what you want—bread. You will see by using this more perfect, or as you would say, more subtle law, I am able to bring forth exactly what I need—bread." And as we stood there spellbound a large loaf of bread was in his hands, nor did the supply stop until there were forty loaves upon the table before us, placed there apparently by Emil himself. He remarked, "You see there is sufficient for all; if not sufficient, more can be supplied until there is enough and to spare." We all ate the bread and pronounced it good.

Emil continued, "When Jesus at Galilee asked Philip, 'Whence shall we buy bread?' He did this to try him, for within Himself He knew full well there was no necessity to buy the bread needed to feed the assembled multitude nor to secure it through the material market then in existence. He saw the opportunity to prove to His disciples the power of bread leavened or increased by the Spirit. How often man in the mortal concept thinks as did Philip! He was calculating, as human consciousness is calculating today, from the visible supply on hand — thinking he had only so much bread or so much supply or so much money with which to buy. Jesus recognized that the one in Christ Consciousness knows no limitation. He then, in Christ Consciousness, looked to God as the source and creator of all and gave thanks for the power and substance right at hand to fill every want. He then broke and distributed, through His disciples, to those in outer need until the need was supplied and there remained twelve baskets over. Jesus never depended on the over-supply of another to fill His need nor the need of another; but He taught that our supply is right at hand in Universal Substance where all supply exists and all we need do is to create it or bring it forth. Just so when Elisha multiplied the widow's oil. He did not apply to someone having an over-abundance of oil, for had he done this the supply would have been limited. He contacted the Universal and the only limit to the supply was that all the vessels were filled.

The supply could have flowed on until this day had there been vessels to receive it.

"This is not hypnotism. None of you feel that you are in any way under a hypnotic spell. Let me say that the only hypnotism is the self-hypnotism of believing that each and every one can not do the perfect works of God, and create the desired condition or thing. For is not the need itself the desire to create? Instead of unfolding and creating as God wills us to create, you fold up in your little shells and say, 'I can't,' and you hypnotize yourselves into actually believing that you are separate entities apart from God. You simply fall short of your perfect creation or expression. You do not let God express perfectly through you as it is His desire to do. Did not Jesus the Great Master say, 'The works that I do, ye shall do also, and greater works than these shall ye do'? Was it not Jesus' true mission here on earth to show that we, as Sons of God, or man in his true estate, can create as perfectly and as harmoniously as God does? When Jesus commanded the blind man to bathe his eyes in the pool of Siloam, was not this intended to open the eyes of all? All were to see that Jesus was sent by the Father to show us that the Father intended us to create exactly as He creates; all are to do the perfect work as Jesus did by recognizing the Christ in himself and in all.

"I can go one step further. This loaf I just received and held in my hand is consumed as though burned by fire. What happened? I misused the perfect law that brought forth my conception and consumed that which I brought forth, because of my misuse or not using rightly, or righteously, the perfect law which is as exact as music or mathematics or any other so-called natural law. If I persisted in the misuse of the perfect law, it would consume not only that which I create but would consume me, the creator.

"Is the bread really destroyed? We will admit the form is changed for, in place of the loaf, we have a small amount of dust or ashes. Has it not in reality been returned to the Universal Substance from which it sprang? Is it not now in unmanifest form, waiting to be brought again into manifestation? Is this not the way with all forms that go from our sight either by fire or decay or in any other way? Do they not return to the Universal Substance—God—from which they sprang? Is this not the meaning of 'What descends from heaven must ascend into heaven'?

"A short time ago you saw ice formed, without any apparent cause, as you perhaps think of it. Let me say that that is the same as creating the bread. I can use the law to obtain ice as well as bread, just as long as I use either as a benefit to mankind, or as long as I am working in living accord with the law, or expressing as God wishes all to express. It is good for all to make bread, or ice, or any and all things desired; and all must press on to the stage at which they can do these things. Can you not see that by using the highest law, the absolute law of God, you may bring forth that which you need or conceive in mind as your highest idea and thus please God more fully by manifesting more fully, knowing as Jesus did that we are perfect Sons of God?

"Does not this suggest freedom from commercial bondage as well as all other bondage? As I see it, the commercial bondage will, in a few years, become the greatest bondage of all. If it goes on at the rate it is now progressing, it will dominate man, soul and body, and it cannot do otherwise than consume itself and those that are interested in it. There is no question but that the first inception of commercialism was on a high spiritual plane, but materialism was allowed to creep in until the very power used to create is the power that will consume; just as the very power used to create will always consume if not used rightly. Is not the pressing of commercialism and limitations upon us crowding us on to see that we must come up over, or overcome, these conditions? Is not this done by simply realizing that we are to do the perfect works of God, to raise our consciousness to the Christ Consciousness? Is not this what Jesus taught us here on earth? Does not His whole life exemplify this?

"My dear brothers, do you not see that in the beginning there was the Word and the Word was with God? At this time, everything to be formed later was in unmanifest form in the Universal Mind Substance — or as expressed by some, in chaos. This word in the original was actuality. This word, chaos, is misinterpreted to mean a turbulent or warring state, instead of the deep, spiritual state of actuality, always awaiting a definite, creative, spoken word through which it can spring forth into manifest form.

"When God Principle desired to bring forth the world out of Universal Mind Substance, God was quiet and contemplative. In other words, God saw an ideal world; He held in mind that substance of which the world was to be formed a sufficient time to lower its vibration; then He spoke the Word and the world was formed — or, as we might say, God visualized a mental pattern or mold into which could flow the substance needed to make the world and it came forth a perfect form, built upon the pattern which was held in consciousness.

"All these things might have been thought of by God, Infinite Power. He might have wished during an indefinite time that they were formed and made

[46]

visible. Had not the definite spoken word been put forth into the formless ether, nothing would have been created or brought forth into visible form. In order to establish in visible results the thought and desires of even an Infinite Omnipotent Creator and bring orderly forms out of actuality, it took the definite, positive 'Let there be.' So must we take the definite step.

"God is holding the ideal perfect world in mind in every detail and it is bound to come forth as a heaven or perfect home where all His children, all His creatures, and all His creations may dwell in peace and harmony. This is the perfect world that God saw in the beginning and the one He is thinking into existence right now, and the time of its manifestation lies in our acceptance of it. When we can come to the one place and know that we are all one, one man, and know that we are all members of God's body as much as one member of our body is a part of the whole body, then we are in, and of, God's kingdom, heaven here on earth, now.

"To make this manifest, realize that there is nothing material in heaven. All is spiritual. Realize that heaven is a perfect state of consciousness, a perfect world here on earth now, and all we need to do is to accept it. It is here all about us, waiting for us to open the inner eye. Through that eye our bodies shall be made light, the light which is neither of the sun nor moon but of the Father; and the Father is right here in the very innermost part of our being. We must sufficiently realize that there is nothing material, that all is spiritual. Then we must think of that wonderful God-given spiritual world which is right here now if we can realize it.

"Do you not see that God created all in this way? Did not God first become quiet and contemplative and see the light? Then He said, 'Let there be light,' and it was so. In the same way He said, 'Let there be a firmament,' and it was so; and likewise with other creations, He held each form or ideal steadfast in consciousness, then spoke the word, and the ideal was brought forth. Just so with man. God said, 'Let us make man in Our image, after Our likeness and give him dominion over all.' God, all good, created all things good; man the greatest and last, with full dominion over all. Then man saw only good, and all was good until man separated himself from God and saw duality, or two. Then he, by his thought, created two, one good and the other the opposite; for if there were two, they would be opposite — good and evil. Thus evil came through man's perfect power to express or bring forth that which he gazed upon. If man had not seen evil, evil would have been given no power of expression. Only the good would have been expressed and we would be as perfect as God sees us today. Would not heaven always have been on earth as God sees it and as we must all see it to make it manifest? Jesus had a perfect right to say that He came from heaven; for did not all come from heaven, the great Universal Mind Substance?

"Since man was created in the image and likeness of God, did not God give man the power to create exactly as He creates? And does not God expect man to use that power as freely as He uses it — and in exactly the same way? By first perceiving the need; then conceiving the good, the ideal, with which to fill the mold that we hold in consciousness and which is to be filled from the Universal Mind Substance; then sending forth the word that it is filled; that it is so, and it is good.

"Jesus, when He was crucified, gave His flesh, the outer, what we see of the body, to prove that there is really a deeper or spiritual body; and it is this spiritual body that He manifested when He came forth from the tomb. This is the body of which He spoke when He said, 'Destroy this temple and in three days I will raise it up.' He did this to show us we have the same spiritual body and that we can do all the works He did. There is no question that if Jesus had wished to do so, He could have saved Himself. There is no doubt but that He saw there was a great change taking place in His body. He also saw that those about Him were not able to see that they also could bring forth the spiritual body, as He was attempting to have them see. They still looked to the personal and He saw that if He brought forth the spiritual body without some decided change, the people would not be able to discern between the material and the spiritual; so He adopted the way of the crucifixion to bring about the change.

"Truly is not this the Christ in man, which the Great Master, Jesus, whom we all love and reverence, came to show? Did He not unfold His life here on earth to show us the perfect way to God? Can we do other than love this perfect ideal way when we once see it, whether it be planting seed, making bread, or doing the million and one things necessary to human existence? Are not these acts mere lessons carrying us on to our unfoldment? Some day we are to realize that we are truly Sons of God, not servants; that as Sons we can and do have all that the Father has and that we can use it just as freely as our Father does.

"I admit this takes a mighty faith at first; one that usually must be taken step by step and must be practiced faithfully like music or mathematics, until we come to the place of knowing. Then we are grandly, beautifully free. Could there be a better, truer example of this life than that of Jesus? Can you not recognize the power that is in His name, Jesus, the Christ made manifest, or God manifesting through the flesh man? Jesus came to the place where He relied wholly upon His deep knowledge or understanding of God and this is how He did His mighty works. He did not rely upon His own will power or upon strong, concentrated thoughts. Neither must we rely upon our own will power nor strong, concentrated thoughts, but upon the will of God. ''Tis not my will, but Thine, O God, be done.' Will to do the will of God. Do you not think that Jesus willed in all things to do the will of God or to do what God willed Him to do?

"You will note that very often Jesus is referred to as going into a high mountain. Whether He physically ascended a high mountain or not, I do not know. This I do know, that we must all ascend to the heights, the very highest in consciousness to receive our illumination. This height means the very top of the head and there, if the faculty is not developed, we must develop it by spiritual thoughts. Then from the heart, the love center, we must let love flow forth to balance all and when this is done the Christ is revealed. The son of man perceives that he is the Son of God, the only begotten Son, in whom the Father is well pleased. Then with constant love, we must realize this for all.

"Just stop and think deeply for a moment and realize the countless number of the grains of sand of the seashore; the countless number of drops of water that go to make up the waters of the earth; the countless number of life forms in the waters of the earth. Then realize the countless number of rock particles that are contained in the whole earth; the countless number of trees, plants, flowers, and shrubs upon the earth; the countless number of forms of animal life upon the earth. Realize that all are the outpicturing of the ideal held in the great universal mind of God; that they all contain the one life, the life of God. Then think of the countless

[50]

number of souls born upon this earth. Then realize that each soul is a perfect outpictured ideal image of God as God sees Himself; that each soul is given the same power, expression, and dominion over all that God Himself has. Do you not think that God wills or wishes man to unfold these God-like or God-given qualities and to do the works that God does through the inheritance given man by the Father, the one great, Universal Mind in all, through all, and above all? Then realize that each person is an expression or pressing out (from the unseen, the Spirit) into visible form, a form through which God loves to express. When we can realize and accept this, we can truly say as Jesus did, 'Behold a Christ is here.' It is in this way that He attained His mastery over the worldly or flesh self. He recognized, claimed, and accepted His divinity, then lived the life just as we must do."

CHAPTER VIII

AFTER a delay of eight days, we broke camp on Monday morning and proceeded on our way. The afternoon of the third day out, we came to the bank of a larger river. The stream was about two thousand feet wide, running bank-full, and the current was at least ten miles per hour. We were told that this stream, in ordinary times, could be crossed at this place without any inconvenience.

We decided to camp until morning and observe the rise and fall of the water. We were informed that we would be able to cross by bridge farther up stream, but to reach this bridge would necessitate a detour of at least four days' hard travel. We felt that if the water was receding, it would be better to wait a few days rather than undertake the long detour. It had been demonstrated to us that we need not take any thought as to our provisions for, from the day already referred to, when our provisions were exhausted the whole company, consisting of over three hundred persons, had been supplied with an abundance of provisions from the invisible, as we called it. This supply was maintained for sixty-four days, until we returned to the village from which we started. Thus far, none of us had any idea of the true significance or meaning of the things we were experiencing. Neither were we able to see that these things were performed by definite law, a law that all can use.

When we were assembled for breakfast next morning, we found five strangers in camp. They were introduced and it was mentioned that they were from a party that was camped on the other side of the stream and were returning from the village of our destination. We thought very little of this at the time, as we naturally supposed they had found a boat and had crossed in it. One of our party said, "If these people have a boat, why can we not use it to cross the stream?" I think all of us saw this as a way out of our difficulty; but we were told that there was no boat as the crossing was not thought to be of sufficient importance to maintain one.

After finishing breakfast that morning we were all assembled on the banks of the stream. We noticed that Emil, Jast, and Neprow with four others of our party were talking with the five strangers. Jast came to us and said they would like to cross with the others to the camp on the other side of the stream as they had decided to wait until the next morning to see if the water showed signs of receding. Of course, our curiosity was aroused and we thought it rather foolhardy to attempt to swim a stream as swift as the one before us just to make a friendly call upon a neighbor. We felt that swimming was the only way the crossing could be accomplished.

When Jast rejoined the group, the twelve, fully dressed, walked to the bank of the stream, and with the utmost composure stepped on the water, not into it. I never shall forget my feelings as I saw each of those twelve men step from solid ground upon the running water. I held my breath, expecting, of course, to see them plunge beneath and disappear. I found afterwards that that was the thought of all our party. At the time, I think each of us held his breath until they were all past midstream, so astonished were we to see those twelve men walking calmly across the surface of the stream without the least inconvenience and not sinking below the soles of their sandals. When they stepped from the water to the farther bank I felt that tons of weight had been lifted off my shoulders and I believe this was the feeling of every one of our party, judging from the sighs of relief as the last man stepped ashore. It certainly was an experience that words fail to describe. The seven belonging to our party returned for lunch. While the excitement was not so intense at the second crossing, every one of us breathed more freely when the seven were safe ashore again. Not one of our party had left the bank of the stream that forenoon. There was very little discussion regarding what we had witnessed, so engrossed were we with our own thoughts.

It was decided that afternoon that we would be obliged to make the detour to the bridge in order to cross the stream. We were up early next morning ready to proceed on the long detour. Before we started, fifty-two of the company walked calmly down to the stream and across, the same as the twelve had done the day before. We were told that we would be able to cross with them, but none of us had the faith to make the attempt. Jast and Neprow insisted upon accompanying us. We attempted to dissuade them, saying that we could follow along with the others, thus saving them the inconvenience. They were unyielding and stayed with us, saying that it was absolutely no inconvenience to them.

The subject of conversation and thought during the four days it took us to join those that had crossed was the remarkable things we had seen accomplished during the short time we had been with those wonderful people. The second day the company was toiling up the steep side of a mountain with the hot sun pouring down upon us when our Chief, who had said but little during the last two days, suddenly remarked, "Boys, why is it that man is obliged to crawl and grovel over this earth?" We answered in chorus that he had voiced our thoughts exactly.

He went on to say, "How is it, if a few are able to

do the things we have seen accomplished, that all men cannot accomplish the same things? How is it that man is content to crawl, and not only content to crawl but is obliged to do so? If man was given dominion over all things, he was certainly given power to fly above the birds. If this is his dominion why has he not asserted this dominion long ago? The fault must certainly be in man's own mind. This must all have come about by man's own mortal concept of himself. He has only been able, in his own mind, to see himself crawling; thus he has only been able to crawl."

Then Jast took up the thought and said, "You are perfectly right, it is all in man's consciousness. He is limited or unlimited, bound or free, just as he thinks. Do you think that the men you saw walk across the stream yesterday to save themselves the inconvenience of this trip are in any way special creations any more than you are? No. They are not created in any way different from you. They do not have one atom more power than you were created with. They have, by the right use of their thought forces, developed their God-given power. The things you have seen accomplished while you have been with us, you, yourselves, can accomplish just as fully and freely. The things you have seen are accomplished in accord with definite law and every human being can use the law if he will."

The talk ended here and we went on and joined the fifty-two who had crossed, then proceeded to the village.

CHAPTER IX

LOCATED in this village was The Healing Temple. It is claimed that only words of Life, Love, and Peace have been given expression in this temple since its erection, and the vibrations are so potent that nearly all who pass through the temple are instantly healed. It is also claimed the words of Life, Love, and Peace have been used and sent out so long from this temple and the vibrations emanating from them are so strong that, should words of inharmony and imperfection be used at any time, they would have no power. We were told that this is an illustration of what takes place in man. If he would practice sending forth words of Life, Love, Harmony, Peace, and Perfection he would in a short time not be able to utter an inharmonious word. We attempted to use inharmonious words and found in each instance that we could not even utter them.

This temple was the destination of those of the company who were seeking healing. It is the custom for the Masters who are in the vicinity to congregate at this village at certain intervals for a season of devotion and instruction to those who wish to avail themselves of the opportunity. The temple is dedicated entirely to healing and is open to the people at all times. As it is not always possible for the people to reach the Masters, the Masters encourage the people to go to the temple for healing. This is the reason they do not heal those that congregate for the pilgrimages. They accompany the pilgrims to show the people that they are no different than themselves, that all have the same God-given power within. I suspect that when they crossed the river that morning they did it to show that they could rise above any emergency and that we should also rise above any emergency.

In places not accessible to this temple all who come to the Masters for help are greatly benefited. Of course, there are the curious and those who do not believe that do not seem to receive any help. We witnessed a number of assemblages of from two hundred to two thousand people and all those desiring healing were healed. A great many told us they were healed by declaring silently that they desired to be made whole. We had the opportunity to observe a large number of those healed at different times and we found that about ninety per cent of these healings were permanent, while all the healings in the temple seemed to be permanent. It was explained that the temple is a concrete thing located in one place, representing the God center, the Christ in the individual — just as all churches should typify this God, or Christ center, in the individual — and that it is always accessible to those desiring to go there. They could go to the temple as often as they chose and stay as long as they wished. The ideal is thus formed in the minds of those who come to it and the ideal becomes fixed in mind.

Emil said, "Right here comes the suggestion that has led to the idolatry of the past. Men sought to grave in wood or stone, gold, silver or brass the image of that which they idealized but any idol can only imperfectly picture the ideal. The image, the idol, is no sooner formed than men become conscious that the ideal surpasses the idol and they are shown that they must gaze upon love and idealize for themselves that which they wish to bring forth from the within, instead of graving any idol in outer form of the ideal they would express. A later form of idolatry is to idealize the personality of the one who expresses our ideal. We should idealize the ideal

[57]

which he expresses and not the personality which expresses it. This is true even of so great a person as Jesus. Thus, Jesus chose to go away when He saw the people were idealizing His personality instead of the ideal which He represented. They sought to make Him their King, only realizing that He could supply them with every outer need, not recognizing that they within themselves had the power to supply their every need and that this they must do, as He, Himself, had done. He said, 'It is expedient that I go away for if I do not go, the Comforter will not come,' meaning that as long as they looked to His personality they would not recognize their own powers. For they must look within, within their very selves.

"Another may teach or tell you, but you of yourselves must do the work, for if you look to another, you build the idol instead of bringing forth the ideal."

We witnessed wonderful healings. Some sufferers only walked through the temple and were healed. Others spent considerable time there. At no time did we see anyone officiate as the vibrations of the spoken word were so potent that all who came within the influence were benefited. We saw one man, who was suffering from ossification, carried into the temple and completely healed. Inside of an hour he walked, completely restored. He afterwards worked for our party for four months. Another man who had lost the fingers of his hand had them completely restored. A little child with withered limbs and distorted body was instantly healed and walked out of the temple. Cases of leprosy, blindness, deafness, and many other diseases were cured instantly. In fact, all who went into the temple were healed. We had the opportunity to observe at intervals, two to three years afterward, a number of those that were healed at this time and the healing was permanent. We were told that if the healing was not permanent and the infirmity returned, it was on account of the lack of the true spiritual realization of the individual.

CHAPTER X

WHEN we returned to headquarters we found all in readiness for crossing the mountains. After a day's rest and a change of porters and animals, we started on the second stage of our journey, this time actually to cross the Himalayas. The happenings of the next twenty days were of but passing interest.

Emil talked to us on the realization of the Christ Consciousness. He said, "It is through the power of our own mind or thought action that we are able to bring forth or realize the Christ Consciousness. Through the power or process of thought we can transmute and evolve our bodies, or our outer conditions and surroundings, through recognition of this Christ Consciousness within ourselves, so that we will never experience death nor any change called death. This is done wholly through man's power to vizualize, idealize, conceive, and bring forth that which he gazes upon. This is done by first knowing or perceiving or having faith that the Christ is within ourselves; seeing the true meaning of Jesus' teaching; holding our body one with God, made in the image and likeness of God and merging that body into the perfect God body just as God sees us. We have idealized, conceived, and brought forth into manifestation the perfect God body. We are 'born again' truly of and in the Spirit Kingdom of God.

"It is in this way that we can return all things to the Universal Mind Substance, from which they sprang, and bring them back or return them perfect into outer form or manifestation. Then, by holding them in their pure, spiritual, perfect state, the vibrations are lowered and the things we wish to create come forth in perfect form. In this way we can take every false belief, every old condition, every sin, all of our past life — it does not matter what it has been, how good or seeming bad, it does not matter what mountain of false belief or doubt and unbelief or fear we or anyone else have erected about us or in our paths — and we can say to them all, 'I now return you to the great ocean of Universal Mind Substance, from which all things come forth and where all is perfection, and from which you sprang, there to be again resolved into the elements from which you were created. I now return you or bring you back from that pure substance as perfect and pure as God sees you and hold you always in that absolute perfection.' We can say to ourselves, 'I now realize, in the old order of things, that I brought you forth imperfectly and you manifest imperfectly. Realizing the Truth, I now bring you forth perfect as God sees you. You are reborn perfect and "it is so".' We must realize that the inner alchemist, God within, has taken hold of this and has transmuted, refined, and perfected that which seemed imperfect, that which we brought forth and are now returning. We should realize that it is refined, perfected, and transmuted just as our own bodies are refined, perfected, and returned to us as God's body, joyously perfect, beautifully free. Finally, we should realize that this is the perfect Christ Consciousness in all and for all. This is 'Hid with Christ in God.'"

The morning of July 4th found us at the summit of the pass. Emil had told us the evening before that he felt we had earned a holiday and that he saw no more fitting time than the Fourth to celebrate.

At breakfast Emil began by saying, "This is the Fourth of July, the day you celebrate the birth of your independence. How fittingly expressive is this day!

"I feel that all of you must have more or less confidence in us; therefore, I am going to speak freely. In a few days we shall be able to prove to you conclusively that the statements I am making are true.

"We love to call your country 'America,' and all of its inhabitants, 'Americans.' You will never know the joy these few moments bring to me, on this day of such import, to be able to talk with you and see eye to eye with a small group of Americans who were, with one exception, born in that great land. Let me say that it has been the privilege of some of us to have beheld your country long before Columbus started on the memorable expedition. There had been other attempts at discovery but they had come to naught. Why? Simply because of the absence of that one God-given quality—faith. The one who had the courage and faith to see and carry out the vision had not yet awakened. The moment that soul awoke to the realization that the earth was round and there must be land on the other side equal to that already known, we could see that another great historical epoch had begun to unfold.

"Who but the great Omnipotent One, who sees all things, could have awakened that little grain of faith in the soul of Columbus? What were his first words as he stood before the Queen that day, not recognizing the higher power? 'Dear Queen, I am firmly convinced that the earth is round and I wish to sail forth and prove it.' I do not know whether you recognize it but those words were God-inspired and Columbus was recognized as one who had the determination to carry out what he undertook.

"Then the long sequence of events started to unfold which was shown us years before, not in its entirety, but enough so that we have been able to follow. Of course we dreamed of the almost unbelievable wonders to be accomplished and recorded in the seemingly short span of years has passed, but those of us that have been privileged to live through it now fully realize that far greater wonders are in store for your great nation. We feel that the time has come for your nation to awaken to its true spiritual import and we wish to do all we can to help you to this realization."

It appears that their interest in us was prompted by their great desire to have America accept the Christ Consciousness and realize her possibilities. They know that her inception was truly spiritual and through that fact she is destined to be a leader in the spiritual development of the world.

Emil continued, "Think of this made possible by the little seed of faith planted in the consciousness of one man they allowed to develop. What has happened? Can you realize it? Columbus, in his day, was thought to be an impractical dreamer. Are we not all coming to the place where we believe and know that the dreams of yesterday are but the realities of today? For who has accomplished anything who was not a so-called dreamer? In reality, were his visions dreams? Were they not ideals in the Great Universal Mind, God, conceived in the soul of the one who brought them forth as a great Truth? Did he not set forth upon an uncharted sea, visioning clearly in his own consciousness a land beyond? Whether he saw the promise and prominence to be attained by the land, or even the name of America to be given to it, I do not know. In all probability that was left for those that followed to work out. The point is—was it not first a dream or vision? We already see some of the wonders unfolded but we can only visualize the wonders yet to follow as the result of that one vision. In this way we may recount the many visions that have helped to make the world a better place in

[63]

which to live. Is not this the way God manifests or expresses through all? The one that has already brought forth is the one that has the greater faith in God, either consciously or unconsciously. Think of that soul setting out upon what was then an uncharted sea, the hardships, the trials and discouragements, with but one thought uppermost in mind — the goal.

"Then events led on and always up — to the day when that little handful embarked on the Mayflower seeking freedom to worship God in their own way. Think of it — in their own way! Taken in the light of the Spirit and subsequent happenings does the real truth come? Did they not build greater than they thought? Can you not see the hand of the Great Omnipotent One above it all? Then came the dark days when it seemed as though the first Colonies would be snuffed out, but what God has set His hand to must triumph. Still later came the great day of the signing of the Declaration of Independence and choosing either God or oppressor. Who prevailed, who must always prevail? Whether you realize it or not, the struggles of that little body of men in those memorable days and the act of affixing their names to that document is one of the greatest epics since that of the advent of Jesus into the world.

"Then came the strokes of the Independence Bell. Believe it or not, the first strokes of that bell were known to us as truly as if we had been standing beneath it. That bell magnified and sent out the vibrations that emanated from that little center until some day they will penetrate the deepest and darkest corners of the whole earth and thus enlighten the darkest consciousness.

"Look at the trials and vicissitudes that led up to that event. Was not the Great Child born that day? See the great souls that dared to come forth to sponsor the child. Had they lost heart see what might have happened! They did not falter or lose heart. What did happen? This greatest nation of all the earth was born. Her trials and tribulations since bespeak what? Are they not closely allied with the unfoldment of that great soul, Jesus of Nazareth? Cannot those that signed the Declaration of Independence that day be likened unto the Wise Men from the East who saw the Star symbolizing the birth of the Babe in the Manger, the Christ Consciousness in man? Did they not perceive the Star just as truly as those of old?

"Calling to mind the words of that declaration, can you doubt that every word was God-inspired? Stop a moment and think. Is there a parallel in all history? Is there or was there ever a document like it from which it could have been copied? Is there any doubt that it came direct from the Universal Mind Substance? Is there any doubt that it is a part of the great creative plan being brought into manifestation? Is there any doubt that it is a successive stage in the working out of that great plan?

"Is there any question that the watchword *e pluribus unum* (one out of many or unity out of diversity or multiplicity) was adopted during the successive stages of evolution of the Spirit of Truth? It certainly did not emanate mechanically from man's mortal mind. Then the emblematic phrase—*In God We Trust*—does not that show the most sanguine faith or trust in God, the creator of all? Then the choice of the eagle, the bird which represents the highest aspiration, as the emblem. It shows that these men were deeply spiritual or they builded better than they knew. Can you doubt for a moment that all were guided by the whole of the God spirit in creative action? Does it not bespeak that America is destined to be the guide to the whole world?

[65]

"Consider the history of your nation. There is not a parallel in the history of the nations of the whole earth. Can you not see each succeeding step leading up to its fulfillment? Can you believe that there is any other than a Master Mind working out its unfoldment? Can you doubt that it is the Great Omnipotent God guiding its destiny?

"Just as the mustard seed, although it is among the smallest of seeds, has the faith to know that within itself it has the power to express the mustard plant, the greatest of all herbs, for 'when it is grown it becomes a tree and the birds may come and lodge in the branches thereof;' just as a seed knows that within itself it has the power to express the greatest, so must we know that we have the power within ourselves to express the greatest. In giving this parable it was the quality instead of the quantity of faith that Jesus referred to. 'If ye have the faith as a grain of mustard seed (and that faith becomes knowing), ye shall say unto this mountain, "Remove hence to yonder place," and it shall remove, and nothing shall be impossible unto you.' Just so the frailest poppy seed and the mightiest banyan tree, the bulb, the plant, the tree seed, all know that they can express the greatest. Each has an exact picture or representation of what it must express. So must we have an exact picture within ourselves of what we desire to express. Then there must be an inner perfecting wrought by hourly preparation and this perfection will come forth. No flower ever burst into full bloom without this perfecting inner urge. A moment before the bud was confined within the sepal sense of self, but when this inner perfection is complete, the flower bursts forth beautiful.

"As the seed that falls into the ground must first give forth from self in order to grow, develop, and multiply, so must we first give forth from self to unfold. As the seed must first burst its shell in order to grow, so must we burst our shell in order to grow, so must we burst our shell of limitation to begin our growth. When this inner perfection is complete we must come forth beautiful, the same as the flowers. As with an individual so with a nation. Can you not see that with the Christ Consciousness fully developed in such a nation, whatever is undertaken by it or by its people must work out for good to all; for the very root or heart of all government is the consciousness of those governed.

"Great mistakes have been made by your nation in the ongoing because you have not realized your spiritual import and the vast majority are still deep in the material. I fully realize that great souls have guided the destiny of your nation. I also realize how little those great souls have been appreciated until they have passed on. The way has been jagged and bushy, a hard way, because man in his limited concept, thus far, let only the mortal concept build the way. See what wonders he has accomplished! But see what wonders could have been accomplished had the fuller, deeper spiritual meaning been understood and applied. In other words, had the Christ been placed at the helm of your Ship of State, and could all have known the truth as Jesus did—that the Christ is in every man and that all are one—what wonders would stand revealed today. I behold the same glory yet to be, as soon as the deep spiritual meaning of *e pluribus unum* is understood. Do you not realize that it is one of the first great laws of God, the one expressing through the many, one of all and for all?

"Consider every nation that has been founded. Those founded on true spiritual perception have endured the longest and would have endured forever, had not materialism been allowed to creep in and gradually undermine the whole structure until they fell by their own abnormal weight or were consumed by the misuse of the law that gave them birth. By the fall of each, what has happened? The Principle, or God part, was preserved until in each succeeding failure we can trace a gradual rise or upward ongoing in each successive stage, until finally all must end in God, One of Many. My brothers, it does not need a prophet to bring you to a realization of this.

"See what a nation Spain was at the time Columbus set forth on his voyage of discovery, and for a short time afterwards, and see now what is happening. In a short time she will be at war with her own child. Then you will see what a helpless, impotent nation she is, hardly able to totter into a good fight or out of a poor one. To what can you attribute her impotency? Is it utter devitalization? Is it not always thus with a nation or an individual? When the body form or structure has been satiated, whether by greed or passion, the results are the same. There may be a time of seeming prosperity and success, but this is short-lived; then the decrepit, emaciated, and wasted form bears evidence, as does the halting, uncertain step of the old. Whereas, had they conserved and developed their spiritual power they would be as resilient and buoyant at five hundred, five thousand, or ten thousand years, or eternally, as they were in the heyday of their ascendancy.

"How we look forward to the age which is dawning, the Age of Crystal, the pure, white light of dawn gradually breaking, and in a short space of time all will see the full blaze and glory of this approaching day. Then there will be no darkness, no limitation. Does not this suggest that there must be eternal progress? If not, all must return to that from which it sprang, the Universal Substance. All must progress

[68]

or go back; there is no halfway point, no stopping place. When your nation does recognize its true estate, or mission, and join hands with Spirit and expresses as God wishes it to express, or lets the Spirit unfold from within; we can see for your great nation a marvel far transcending the power of any human tongue to describe.

"There is no question but that it took the great strong beak and talons of the eagle to hold your nation together during its development; but when the true spiritual light comes, it will be seen that the dove is mightier than the eagle, and the dove will protect what the eagle now guards. Look at the words on the coin you send into every avenue of the world trade—*In God We Trust* and *e pluribus unum,* one composed of many, the very slogan of Spirit when the dove replaces the eagle on the life medium of such a nation."

The talk ended here and Emil went on to say that he would leave us for a short time as he wished to go to meet some of the others who were assembling in a village two hundred miles away. He said he would rejoin us at a small village sixty miles away, at which we would arrive in about four days. He then disappeared and, with four others, joined us four days later in a small village on the frontier.

CHAPTER XI

THE day we arrived at this village was very rainy and we were all drenched to the skin. We were assigned to very comfortable quarters, with a large comfortably furnished room that we could use as a dining and sitting room. This room was exceedingly warm and cheery and one of our party asked where the heat came from. We all looked around but could not find a stove or any place where the heat came from, although there was a warm glow that was very noticeable. We wondered at this but did not say much as we were becoming accustomed to surprises and were quite certain that all would be made plain later on.

We had just seated ourselves at the dinner table when Emil and the four came in. We did not know where they came from. They all appeared at one end of the room simultaneously and at the end of the room where there were no openings. They appeared there without any noise or display and walked quietly to the table where Emil introduced the others. Then they sat down as though perfectly at home. Before we realized it the table was filled with good things to eat but no meat. These people do not eat meat nor anything that has had conscious life.

After the meal was finished and we were sitting around the table, one of our party asked how the room was warmed. Emil said, "The warmth that you feel in this room comes from a force that we are all able to contact and use. This force or power is higher than any of your mechanical force or power but can be contacted by man and used as light, heat, and power even to the driving of all mechanical appliances. It is what we call a universal force. If you were to contact and use this force, you would call it perpetual motion. We call it Universal Power, God Power, supplied by the Father to work for all His children. It will turn and move every mechanical device, furnish transportation without the consumption of fuel in any way, and will also furnish light and heat. It is everywhere present without money or price and can be contacted and used by all."

One of our party asked if the food had been prepared by this force. We were told that the food came prepared as we had eaten it, direct from the Universal, just the same as the bread and the other provisions had been supplied heretofore.

We were then invited by Emil to accompany the group to their home, about two hundred miles distant, where we would meet Emil's mother. He went on to say, "My mother is one who has so perfected her body that she was able to take it with her and go on and receive the highest teachings. Therefore she is living in the invisible at all times. She is doing this from choice as she wishes to receive the highest; and by receiving the highest teaching she is able to greatly assist us. In order to make this clear to you, I might say that she has gone on until she has reached the Celestial Realm, as you would call it, the place where Jesus is. This place is sometimes called the Seventh Heaven. To you I suppose this suggests the mystery of mysteries. Let me say that there is no mystery about it. It is a place in consciousness where every mystery is revealed. Those who have reached that state of consciousness are outside the mortal vision but they can return and converse and teach those who are receptive. They can come in their own bodies, for they have so perfected their bodies that they can go where they will with them. They are able to return to earth without reincarnation. Those who have passed through death are obliged to be reincarnated in order to return to earth with a body. This body was given to us as a spiritual, perfect body and we must so see and keep the body in order to retain it. Those who have left the body and have gone on in spirit now realize that they must again take up a body and go on and perfect it."

It was arranged, before leaving the table that evening, that the party should divide into five groups, each group in charge of one of the five that had appeared in the room and taken dinner with us. This would enable us to cover a larger field and would greatly facilitate our work; and at the same time it would enable us to verify such things as traveling in the invisible and thought transference. This plan would give us at least two of our men in each party and one of the five as leader. We would be quite widely separated, yet we were to keep in touch through those who were so greatly befriending us and giving us every opportunity to prove their work.

CHAPTER XII

T HE next day all details were arranged and three of our party, including myself, were to accompany Emil and Jast. The morning following found each party with its guide and attendants all ready to depart in different directions, with the understanding that we should carefully observe and record all that occurred, and should meet sixty days later at Emil's home in the village just spoken of, two hundred miles distant. We were to keep in communication with each other through our friends. This was accomplished each evening by these friends conversing with each other or traveling back and forth from party to party. If we wished to communicate with our Chief or with any other member of our party, all we need do was to give our message to our friends and in an incredibly short time, we would have the answer. In giving these messages, each would write them out in full and note the time to the minute on each message; then when the answer came we would do the same. When we came together again, we compared notes and found that all notes corresponded. Aside from this our friends would travel from one camp to another and converse with us. We kept accurate records of these appearances and disappearances; also we noted the time, the place, and the conversations and all checked fully when we compared notes later.

At times after this we were widely separated; one party would be in Persia, one in China, one in Tibet, one in Mongolia, and one in India, always accompanied by our friends. At times they traveled in the invisible, as we called it, distances as great as one thousand miles and kept us informed as to the happenings and progress in each camp.

The destination of the party to which I was assigned proved to be a small village to the south-west, located on an elevated plateau well up in the foothills of the Himalayas and about eighty miles from our starting point. We did not take any provisions for the trip but we were amply provided for at all times and had very comfortable quarters. We arrived at our destination early in the afternoon of the fifth day, were greeted by a delegation of villagers, and shown to comfortable quarters.

We noted that the villagers treated Emil and Jast with the utmost reverence. We were told that Emil had never visited the village but that Jast had been there before. The occasion of his first visit was in response to a call for help to rescue three villagers from the fierce snow-men that inhabit some of the wildest parts of the Himalayas. This present visit was in response to a similar call and also to minister to the sick who could not leave the village. These so-called snow-men are outcasts and renegades who have lived in the snow and ice regions of the mountains until they have developed a tribe that is able to live in the mountain fastnesses without contact with any form of civilization. Though not numerous, they are very fierce and warlike and, at times, capture and torture those who are unfortunate enough to fall into their hands. It proved that four of the villagers had been captured by these wild snowmen. The villagers, being at their wits' end to know what to do, had sent out a messenger to get in touch with Jast and he had come to the rescue, bringing Emil and us along.

Of course we were all excited, thinking we were to get sight of these wild people, whom we had heard of but supposed did not exist. We at first believed that

[74]

a rescue party would be organized and we would be allowed to join, but these hopes were shattered when Emil announced that he and Jast would go alone and that they would go immediately.

In a few moments they disappeared and did not return until the second evening, with the four captives, who told weird tales of their adventures and of the strange people that had captured them. It seems that these strange snow-people go entirely naked, that their bodies have become covered with hair like that of a wild animal, and that they can withstand the intense cold of the mountain altitudes. They are said to move over the ground very swiftly; in fact, it is claimed that they are able to pursue and capture the wild animals that live in the region that they inhabit. These wild people call the Masters, "The Men from the Sun," and when the Masters go among them for the prisoners they do not resist. We were also told that the Masters had made a number of attempts to reach these wild people but these attempts had come to naught because of the fear in which the people held them. It is said that if the Masters do go among them, the snow-men will not eat or sleep, but stay in the open night and day, so great is their fear. These people have lost all contact with civilization, even forgetting that they had ever contacted other races or that they are the descendants from them, so far have they separated themselves from others.

We were able to get Emil and Jast to say but little about this strange wild tribe, nor could we influence them to take us to them. When we questioned, the only comment was, "They are God's children, the same as we are, only they have lived so long in hatred and fear of their fellow-men and they have so developed the hatred and fear faculty that they have isolated themselves from their fellow-men to such an extent that they have completely forgotten they are descendants of the human family, and think themselves the wild creatures they appear to be. They have gone on in this way until they have even lost the instinct of the wild creatures, for the wild creature knows by instinct when a human being loves it and it will respond to that love. All we can say is that man brings forth that which he gazes upon and separates himself from God and man, and in this way he can go lower than the animal. It would serve no purpose to take you among them. It would, instead, harm those people. We are in hopes some day to find some one among them who will be receptive to our teaching and in this way reach them all."

We were told that if we wished to make the attempt to see these strange people on our own initiative, we were at liberty to do so; that the Masters could no doubt protect us from any harm and, if we should be taken prisoners, they could in all probability secure our release.

We found that evening we were scheduled to leave the next day for a very ancient temple about thirty-five miles from the village where we were then stopping. My two companions decided they would forego seeing the temple and try to get a closer view of the wild men. They attempted to influence two of the villagers to go with them, but in this they met flat refusal, for none of the villagers would leave the village so long as they thought the wild men were around. My friends decided to attempt it alone so, after receiving instructions from Emil and Jast as to the trail and general direction, they strapped on their side-arms and made ready to start. Before they left, Emil and Jast had exacted a promise from them that they would shoot to kill only as a last resort. They may shoot to frighten as much as they pleased but they must give their word that if they killed it would be the last extremity.

I was surprised that we had even a 45 Colt with us as we had not carried firearms about us. I had discarded mine long ago and did not know where they were. It so happened that one of the coolies that helped to look after our wants had put two pistols in the luggage and they had not been removed.

CHAPTER XIII

EMIL, Jast and I started out later in the day to go to the temple and arrived there the next day at 5:30 in the evening. We found two elderly men in charge and I was made comfortable for the night. The temple is located on a high mountain peak, is built of rough stone, and is said to be over twelve thousand years old. It is in a perfect state of preservation and repair. It is one of the first temples erected by the Siddha teachers and was erected by them as a place where they could go and have perfect silence. The site could not have been better chosen. It is on the highest peak in that part of the mountains; the elevation above sea level is 10,900 feet and it is over 5000 feet above the valley floor. The last seven miles it seemed to me the trail was straight up. At times it led over poles that were supported by ropes fastened to boulders above, then thrown over the cliff's side; and these supported the poles that served as a trail. As we walked over these poles, I realized that we were at least six hundred feet in mid-air. At other times we were obliged to climb pole ladders supported by ropes from above. The last ascent was perpendicular for about three hundred feet and was accomplished wholly by pole ladders. When we arrived I felt as if I were on top of the world.

We were up before the sun the next morning and when I stepped out on the roof of that temple I forgot all about the ascent of the night before. The temple was so situated at the edge of a bluff that, when you looked out, you could see nothing for three thousand feet below, and it seemed as if the whole temple were suspended in mid-air. I had consider-

[78]

able difficulty in persuading myself to believe otherwise. In the distance we would see three mountains
upon which, I was told, temples similar to this were
located, but they were so distant I could not make
out the temples with my field glasses. Emil said that
one of the other parties should have reached the
temple on the farthest mountain at about the same
time that we arrived here last evening and that our
Chief was in the party. He said that if I wished to
communicate with him, I might do so, as they were
at the time standing on the roof of the temple a good
deal like we were doing. I took my notebook and
wrote that I was standing on the roof of a temple
10,900 feet above sea level and it seemed to me as if
the temple were suspended in mid-air; that the time
was exactly 4:55 a.m. by my watch; and the day was
Saturday, August 2. Emil read this message and
stood silent a moment; then the answer came: "Time
5:01 a.m. by my watch; place, suspended in mid-air,
8400 feet above sea level; date, Saturday, August 2.
View wonderful, but situation most remarkable."

Then Emil said, "If you wish, I will take this note
and bring the answer when I return. I would like to
go and converse with those at the temple if you do
not mind." I gave him the note willingly and he
disappeared. In one hour and forty-five minutes he
returned with a note from the Chief stating that
Emil had arrived there at 5:16 a.m. and that they
were having a wonderful time speculating what
would come next.

We stayed at this temple three days. During that
time Emil visited the other parties, carried notes
from me, and returned with answers from them.

The morning of the fourth day, we prepared to
return to the village where we had left my associates.
I found that Emil and Jast wished to go to another
small village, located in the valley about thirty miles

from where our trail left the valley trail. I suggested that they go and I accompany them. We camped that night at a sheepherder's lodge and were up and started early next morning in order to reach our destination before dark the next day, as we were walking. We were not able to use horses on the trip to the temple and so had left them at the village.

About ten o'clock that morning there came on a heavy electric storm and it looked as if there would be a downpour, but no rain fell. The country through which we were passing was quite heavily wooded and the ground was covered with a heavy, thick, dry grass. The country seemed exceptionally dry. The lightning ignited the grass in a number of places and before we knew it, we were virtually surrounded by a forest fire. In a few moments this fire was raging like mad and closing in upon us from three sides with the swiftness of an express train. The smoke was settling down in thick clouds and I became bewildered and panic-stricken. Emil and Jast seemed cool and collected and this reassured me somewhat. They said, "There are two ways of escape. One is to try to get to the next creek, where there is water flowing through a deep canyon. If we can reach this canyon which is about five miles away, we can in all probability make ourselves safe until the fire has burned itself out. The other way is to go on through the fire with us if you can trust us to take you through."

Instantly all fear left me, as I realized that these men had proved true in all emergencies. Throwing myself, as it were, wholly upon their protection, I stepped between them and we proceeded on our way, which seemed to be in the direction the fire was raging the most. Then immediately it seemed as if a great archway opened before us and we went on

[80]

directly through that fire, without the least inconvenience, either from smoke or heat, or from the burning brands strewn along the trail under our feet. There were at least six miles of this fire-swept area that we passed through. It seemed to me as if we were as calmly walking along that trail as though there were no fire raging around. This went on until we crossed a small stream and then were out of the fire.

While we were going through the fire, Emil said to me, "Can you not see how easy it is to use God's higher law to replace a lower one when you really need the higher? We have now raised the vibrations of our bodies to a higher vibration than that of the fire and the fire does not harm us. If senses mortal could see us now, they would think we had disappeared, when in reality our identity is as it has always been. In reality we actually see no difference. It is the concept of the mortal senses that loses contact with us. Could they see us as we are, no doubt they would think we had ascended. In reality that is what happens. We do ascend to a plane of consciousness where the mortal does lose contact with us. All can do the same as we are doing. We are using a law given us by the Father to use. We are able to use this law to convey our bodies through any space. This is the law we are using when you see us appear and disappear or, as you call it, annihilate space. We simply overcome difficulties by raising our consciousness above them and in this way we are able to overcome or to come up over all limitations that man in mortal consciousness has placed upon himself."

To me it had seemed as if we were going over the ground with our feet just touching it. When we were safe across the stream, out of the fire, my first impression was that I had awakened from a deep sleep and had dreamed this, but I gradually awoke to the realization of it all and the real meaning of it began to dawn upon my consciousness. We found a shady place on the bank of the stream, ate our lunch and rested for an hour, then went on to the village.

CHAPTER XIV

THIS village proved very interesting as there are certain well-preserved records that, translated, appear to be conclusive evidence that John the Baptist resided in the village for about five years. We were afterwards to see records and have them translated which seemed to prove conclusively that he resided in this country for about twelve years. We were later on shown records that would seem to prove that John the Baptist sojourned with these people through Tibet, China, Persia, and India for about twenty years. In fact we felt that we were about to follow almost the same route he followed by the records left and preserved. These were of such interest that we returned to the different villages and made an extensive search and found, by comparing the data thus obtained, we could compile quite an accurate map of his travels while with these people. At times these happenings were brought so vividly before us that we could imagine ourselves traveling over the same ground and taking the same route that John did so long ago.

We stopped in this village three days. During these days a wide vista of the past unfolded before me. I could see these teachings going back in the dim past to the very beginning whence all came forth from the one Source or Substance, God. I could see the different offshoots of these teachings being put forth by individuals, each individual adding his concept, each thinking it was his, revealed to him by God or a direct revelation from God to him alone; each feeling that he had the only true message and that he was the only one to give his message to the world. In this way the mortal concepts were mixed with that of

the true revelation intended and diversity and inharmony resulted. Then I could see these people, the
Masters, standing firmly on the rock of true spiri-
tuality, perceiving that man is truly immortal, sinless, deathless, unchanging, eternal, the image and
likeness of God. It seemed to me that further
research must prove that those great people have
preserved and handed this truth down the long ages
in its unadulterated state. They do not claim to have
all there is to give nor do they ask anyone to accept
anything, unless they can prove the words themselves
and do the work the Masters do. They do not claim
any authority save the actual works they do.

After three days I found that Emil and Jast were
ready to return to the village where we had left my
associates. Their mission to the village had been
purely a healing one and there was no doubt but that
they could have made the trip to the temple and this
village in far less time than it had taken us. I was not
able to make the trip as they could; so they made my
way their way.

We arrived at the village and found my associates
waiting for us. Their search for the snow-men had
come to naught. They had searched for five days,
then had given up in disgust and were returning to
the village when their attention was called to what
seemed to be the form of a man outlined against the
sky on a ridge about one mile distant. Before they
could bring their field glasses to bear upon him, he
had so far disappeared that they were able to obtain
only a glimpse. This glimpse gave them the impression of an ape-like form covered with hair. They
hurried to the place but did not find any further
evidence. Although they spent the remainder of that
day searching the surrounding country, they could
find no further evidence and gave up the search.

After hearing my report my associates wanted to

return to the temple but Emil said we would visit a similar one within the next few days and they decided to forego the second trip.

Quite a number of the people from the surrounding country had congregated at the village for healing, as couriers had gone out with the tidings of the rescue of the four who had been captured by the snow-men. We stopped over the next day and attended the assembly and saw some remarkable cures. One young woman about twenty years of age who had had her feet frozen the previous winter had them restored. We could actually see the flesh grow until they were normal and she walked with perfect ease. Two blind people had their sight restored. One of them we were told was born blind. There were a number of minor cases healed.

All seemed profoundly impressed by the work. After the assembly we asked Emil whether there were many converts. He said a great many were really helped and in that way their interest was aroused. They would for a time become workers but the greater part of them soon fell back into their old ways of living, as they found it would be too much exertion to take up the work in earnest. The people nearly all live an easy, carefree life, and there seems to be about one percent of those that profess to believe that are really in earnest. The rest depend entirely upon others to help them when they get into trouble. Right here is where a great deal of their trouble lies. The Masters say they can assist every one that really desires help but they cannot actually do the work for anyone. They can tell others of the abundance in store for them but, to be actually one with and of the abundance, each individual must accept and prove it for himself by actually knowing and doing the works.

CHAPTER XV

W E LEFT the village the next morning and two of the villagers who seemed to have taken up the work accompanied us. The evening of the third day we came to a village about twelve miles from the one where I had been and had looked over the records regarding John the Baptist. I was very anxious to have my associates look over these records, so we decided to stay over, and Jast accompanied us to the village. After going over the records, my associates were deeply impressed and we laid out a plan to map and follow out the travels as outlined in the records.

That evening the Master, who was with the fourth party, spent the night with us. He also brought messages from the first and third parties. He had been born and raised in the village; his forefathers had written the records and they have been in the family from that time on. It was claimed that he was the fifth generation removed from the writer and that not one of the family had experienced death. They had all taken their bodies with them and could return at any time. We asked if it would be too much trouble for the writer of the records to come and talk with us. He said that it would not and we arranged for the interview that evening.

We had been seated but a few moments when a man whom we judged to be about thirty-five appeared suddenly in the room. He was introduced to us and all shook hands with him. We were all spell-bound at his appearance for we had imagined that he would be very old. He was above the medium height, with rugged features, but the kindliest face I had ever looked upon. There was strength of character back of every move. His whole being emanated a light that was beyond our power of comprehension.

Before we were seated Emil, Jast, and the two strangers clasped hands in the center of the room and stood in perfect silence for a few moments. Then all were seated and the one who had appeared in the room so suddenly began by saying, "You have asked for this interview in order to get a better understanding of the documents that have been read and interpreted for you. I will say that these records were made and kept by me; and those referring to that great soul, John the Baptist, which seem to surprise you so greatly, are actual occurrences of the time he was with us here. These records show that he was a man of wide knowledge and wonderful intellect. He perceived that our teaching was true but he apparently never came to the actual realization for, had he done so he would never have seen death. I have sat in this room and heard John and my father converse and it was here that he received much of his teaching. It was here that father passed on and took his body with him and John beheld his passing.

"There are none of my family on father's or mother's side that have not taken their bodies with them in passing. This passing means the perfecting of the body spiritually until one becomes so conscious of the deep spiritual meaning of Life or God that one sees life as God sees it; then one is privileged to receive the highest teaching and from this realm one is able to help all. (We never descend from this realm for those who have reached this place never wish to descend). They know that life is all progress, a going forward; there is no turning back and none wish to do so.

"All are reaching out to help those that are striving for more light and the messages that we are continually sending out into the Universal are being

[87]

interpreted by God's children who are receptive, in every part of the earth today. This is the prime object of reaching this realm or state of consciousness, for we are able to help all in some way. We can and do talk with and instruct those who are receptive and who raise their consciousness, either through their own efforts or the assistance of another. Another cannot do the work for you nor can another carry you along indefinitely. You must decide to do the work for yourself, then do it. Then you are free and self-reliant. When all come into the consciousness, as Jesus did, that the body is a spiritual body and indestructible, and hold themselves in this consciousness, then we shall be able to communicate with all and give out the teaching we have received to a greater number. We are privileged to know that all can accomplish all that we have accomplished and, thereby, solve every problem of life; and that which has been looked upon as difficult and mysterious will be found simple.

"I do not seem any different to you from any other man that you meet every day, neither do I see any difference in you."

We said we thought we could see something far finer in him. He answered, "That is only the mortal as compared with the immortal of man. If you would only look for the God quality and not make any comparison, you would see every human being as you see me; or by looking for the Christ in every face you would bring forth that Christ, or God quality, in all. We make no comparisons; we see only the Christ or God quality in all at all times and in that way we are out of your vision. We see perfection or have perfect vision, while you see imperfection or have imperfect vision. Until you are in contact with someone who is able to instruct you, until you can raise your consciousness where you can see and converse with us as you are now doing, our teaching seems only inspirational in nature. It is not inspiration when we are conversing or attempting to converse with one. This is only in the nature of instruction leading to the point where the true inspiration can be received. It is inspiration only when it comes direct from God and you let God express through you; then you are with us.

"The ideal image of the flower in minutest detail is within the seed and must expand, multiply, unfold, and be wrought into the perfect flower by hourly preparation. When this inner image is complete in minutest detail, the flower comes forth beautiful. Just so God holds the ideal image of every child in mind, the perfect image through which He wishes to express. We can get more out of this ideal way of expression than the flower does if we will but let God express through us in the ideal way He has conceived for us. It is only when we take things into our own hands that the problems and difficulties begin. This is not for one, or a few, this is for all. It has been shown us that we are not different from you. It is a difference in understanding, that is all.

"All the different isms, cults, and creeds, all the different angles of all beliefs, are all good for they will eventually lead their followers to the realization that underneath all there is a deep factor of actuality that has been missed, a deep something that has not been contacted or they have failed to contact that which rightly belongs to them, which they can and should rightfully possess. We see it is this very thing that will eventually drive man to possess all. The very fact that man knows there is something to possess, which can be possessed and which he has not, will goad him on until he has it. It is in this way every step in advance is made in all things. The idea is first pressed out from God's into man's consciousness and he sees there is something ahead if he will but go on. Here man usually blunders and fails to recognize the source from which the idea came; but thinks that it came wholly from within himself. He gets away from God and, instead of letting God express through him the perfection God sees for him, he goes on and expresses in his own way and brings forth imperfectly the thing which should be perfectly wrought or manifest.

"If he should but realize that every idea is a direct, perfect expression from God and, as soon as this idea comes to him, he would immediately make it his ideal to be expressed from God, then take his mortal hands off and let God express through him the perfect way, this ideal would come forth perfect. Here we must realize that God is above the mortal and the mortal cannot help in any way. In this way man would learn in a short time to express perfection. The one great thing man must learn is to get forever through and out of the psychic or mind forces and express directly from God, for all psychic forces are created wholly by man and they are likely to mislead."

CHAPTER XVI

HERE the talk ended with the understanding that all should meet at breakfast. We were up early next morning and ready for breakfast at 6:30. As we left our lodging, we met our friends going in the same direction, walking along and conversing the same as ordinary mortals. They greeted us and we voiced our surprise at meeting them in this way. The reply was, "We are only men the same as you. Why do you persist in looking upon us as different? We are in no way different from you, we have only developed our God-given powers to a greater extent than you."

We then asked, "Why can we not do the works that we have seen you do?" They answered, "Why do not all we contact follow on and do the works? We cannot and do not wish to force our way upon anyone; all are free to live and go the way as they wish to go. We try only to show the easy and simple way, the way we have tried and found very satisfactory."

We went to breakfast and the conversation drifted into the ordinary everyday occurrences. I became lost in wonder. Here were four men sitting opposite us at table. There was one that had lived upon this earth about one thousand years. He had so perfected his body that he was able to take it with him wherever he desired; his body still retained the buoyancy and youth of a man of thirty-five years and this perfection had been completed about two thousand years. Next to him sat a man that was the fifth in line or regular descendant of the family first mentioned. The second had lived upon this earth for more than seven hundred years and his body did not appear to be a day over forty. They were able to converse with us the same as any other men would converse. There was Emil who had lived for over five hundred years and appeared to be about forty; and Jast who was about forty and appeared to be about that age. All were conversing together like brothers with not a hint of superiority, all kindly, simple, and yet well-grounded and logical in every word uttered, with no trace of the mystical or mysterious about them — just plain human beings in daily intercourse with each other. Still I could scarcely realize that it was not all a dream.

After breakfast, when we arose from the table, one of my associates started to pay for the meal. Emil said, "You are our guests here," and held out to the lady in attendance what we thought was an empty hand; but when we looked a second time, there was just the amount of money necessary to pay the bill. We found that our friends did not carry money with them, neither did they depend on others for their supply. When money was needed, it was right at hand, created from the Universal.

We walked out of the house and the man that was with the No. 5 party shook hands with us, saying that he must return to his party, and disappeared. We made a note of the time of his disappearance and afterwards found that he appeared with his party within ten minutes after he had left us.

We spent the day with Emil, Jast, and our friend of the records, as we called him, in wandering over the village and the countryside, our friend recounting in detail many instances which happened in the time of John's sojourn of twelve years in the village. In fact, so vividly were these instances brought to our minds that it seemed as if we were back in the dim past, walking and talking with this great soul, who, to us before this, had seemed but a mythical character conjured from the minds of those who wished to mystify. From that day on, John the Baptist has been a real living character, so real to me it seems as if I can now actually see him walking the streets of the village and countryside and receiving the instruction of those great souls about him, the same as we walked the streets of the village and countryside that day, yet not able to grasp the fundamental truth of it all.

After tramping all day, listening to the most interesting historical occurrences, and hearing records read and translated on the very spot where the incidents took place thousands of years before, we returned to the village just before dark thoroughly tired. The three friends who were with us and had walked every step of the way as we had walked were not showing the least sign of fatigue or weariness. Whereas we were begrimed, dust-laden, and perspiring, they were cool and at ease, their garments were as white and fresh and spotless as when we started out in the morning.

We had noted during all our journeys with these people that none of their clothing became soiled. We had remarked about this a great many times but had received no reply until this evening when, in answer to a remark made, our friend of the records said, "This may seem remarkable to you but it seems far more remarkable to us that one speck of God's created substance adheres to another of God's creations where it is not wanted and where it does not belong. With the right concept this could not happen, for no part of God's substance can be misplaced or placed where it is not wanted."

Then, in an instant we realized that our clothing and bodies were as clean as theirs were. The transformation, for to us it was a transformation, had taken place instantly to all three alike while we stood there. All fatigue left us and we were as refreshed as though we had arisen from bed and had our morning bath.

Here was the answer to all our questions. I believe we retired that night with the deepest feeling of peace we had experienced at any time thus far throughout our sojourn with these people; and our feeling of awe was fast giving place to the deepest love for these simple, kindly hearts that were doing so much for the benefit of mankind, or their brothers, as they call them. We began to look upon them as brothers. They took no credit upon themselves, saying it was God expressing through them, "Of myself I can do nothing. The Father that dwelleth within me, He doeth the works."

CHAPTER XVII

WE WERE up the next morning with every faculty alert with interest and wonder for what that day would reveal. We had begun to look upon each day as a revelation of unfoldment in itself and felt that we were but beginning to realize the deep meaning of the things we were experiencing.

While at breakfast that morning we were told that we would go to a village higher up in the mountains and from that place we would visit the temple that was located on one of the mountains that I had seen while standing on the roof of the temple already described. We were told we would only be able to use our horse for fifteen miles of the journey; and that two of the villagers would go with us that far and would take the horses to another village farther on and care for them until we arrived. We turned our horses over to the two villagers at the appointed place and started to climb to the village up the narrow mountain trail, which at times proved to be steps hewn from the rock. We camped that night at a lodge located on the crest of a point about midway between the place where we had left the horses and the village of our destination.

The keeper of the lodge was fat, old, and jolly; in fact, he was so plump and round that he seemed to roll rather than walk and we could scarcely tell he had eyes. As soon as he recognized Emil he began asking for healing, saying, as we were told afterward, that if he did not get help he would surely die. We were told that he and his forefathers had kept this lodge and served the public for hundreds of years and that he had been in charge about seventy years.

About the time he took over the lodge he was healed of what was called an inherited disease and supposed to be incurable. He had become a very active worker for about two years, then gradually had lost interest and begun to depend upon others to help him out of his difficulties. This had gone on for about twenty years and he had seemed to prosper, seeming to enjoy the best of health, when suddenly he dropped back into his old ways from which he would not make the necessary effort to arouse himself from his lethargy. We found that his case was only a fair example of thousands of others. These people live simply and easily and anything that requires an effort becomes a burden to them very quickly. They soon lose interest and their prayer for help becomes a mechanical sound instead of something uttered with deep meaning or desire.

We were up and on our way early the next morning and four o'clock in the afternoon found us at the village, with the temple of our destination perched on a rocky pinnacle almost overhead. In fact so steep were the walls that the only means of approach was by a basket attached to a rope and let down on a pulley supported by a wooden beam made fast in the rocks. One end of the rope was attached to a windlass and the other was passed over the pulley and fastened to the basket, the basket being let down and pulled up in this manner. The windlass was located in a little room hewn from the solid rock of the ledge that jutted out so that it overhung the rocky walls below. The wooden derrick to which the pulley was attached swung out so that the rope and basket just cleared the ledge, making it possible to haul the load up from below until it cleared; then basket and load were swung in and landed safely on top of the ledge in the little rock room hewed out for the purpose. This rock ledge jutted out over the rock walls below so far that the basket would swing out in midair from fifty to sixty feet as it traveled up and down. At a given signal the basket was lowered; we stepped in and were hauled up, one by one, to the ledge four hundred feet above.

When we were landed upon this ledge we began looking about for some trail leading on up to the temple, the walls of which we could see standing out flush with the wall of rock that still towered five hundred feet above. We were told that we would make the ascent in a similar manner to that already described. As we looked, a derrick arm corresponding to the one on the ledge where we were standing swung out, a rope was let down and attached to the same basket, and we were hauled up, one by one, and landed on the roof of the temple five hundred feet above. I again felt as if we were on top of the world. The temple was located on a rocky pinnacle that stood out nine hundred feet above all of the surrounding mountains. The village we had left nine hundred feet below was located at the summit of a mountain pass used in crossing the Himalayas. We found that this temple was about one thousand feet lower in elevation than the one I had visited with Emil and Jast but it commanded a much wider outlook. From where we stood it seemed as if we could look into infinite space.

We were made comfortable for the night and our three friends told us they were going to visit some of our associates and would take any message we wished to send. We wrote messages, carefully dating them, giving our location and including the time of day. When we handed our friends these messages they shook hands with us, saying they would see us in the morning, and disappeared one by one. We made careful note of the time and of what we had written and found afterward that the messages were at their

[97]

destination within twenty minutes of the time they left our hands.

After eating a hearty supper served by the attendants, we retired for the night, but not to sleep, for our experiences were beginning to make a deep impression upon us. Here we were nearly nine thousand feet in the air, with no human being near us except the attendants, with not a sound except that of our own voices. There did not seem to be a breath of air stirring. One of my associates said, "Do you wonder that they chose the locations of these temples as places of meditation? The stillness is so intense one can fairly feel it. It certainly is a place in which to meditate." He then said he was going outside to have a look around. He went out but returned in a few moments, saying there was a heavy fog and nothing could be seen.

My two associates were soon asleep but I could not sleep; so I arose, dressed, and went out on the roof of the temple and sat down with my feet hanging over the wall. There was just enough moonlight filtering through the fog to eliminate the inky blackness that would have prevailed had not the moon been shining. There was just enough light to reveal the great billowy fog banks rolling by, enough to remind me that I was not suspended in space, that somewhere way down, the earth was as ever, and that the place I was sitting upon was somehow connected with it. Then all of a sudden, it seemed as if I could see a great pathway of light, its rays widening like a fan with the wide part extending toward me; where I was sitting seemed to be in about the center of the ever-widening ray and the central ray was the most brilliant of them all. Each ray seemed to project onward in its course until it illuminated one part of the earth. Each illuminated its own particular portion of the earth until the whole blended in one great white ray. Looking far ahead I could see all gradually converging until they ended in one central point of intense white light, so white that it seemed transparent and crystal. Then, instantly, it seemed as if I stood out in space looking at it all. Looking far, far down the white ray I could see what seemed to be specters of the far-away past marching on and on in ever-increasing numbers but in solid ranks until they reached a certain place; then they separated wider and wider until they filled the whole of the light ray and covered the entire earth. They all seemed to emerge at first from one central white point of light. They seemed to come forth from this point, first one, then just ahead were two, then just ahead of them were four; and so on until they reached the place of wide divergence, where there were about one hundred abreast in solid fan-like array. When they came to the point of wide separation, they suddenly scattered widely and occupied all of the light paths and each marched on more or less alone until they seemed to occupy the whole earth. When they had occupied the whole earth, it seemed the rays had reached their widest expanse. Then they grew gradually narrower and narrower until the rays again converged into the one point from which they first started; the cycle was complete and they entered again one by one. Before they entered they formed in solid array one hundred abreast, gradually closing up until they became one, and that one entered the light alone. I suddenly aroused myself and, thinking that this was rather an unsafe place to be dreaming, I went in and retired.

CHAPTER XVIII

WE HAD asked one of the attendants to call us at the first sign of daybreak; and almost before I knew it, there came a rap at the door. We all bounded out of bed, so eager were we to see the first break of day from our lofty perch. We were dressed in no time and went rushing out on the roof like three eager school boys. In fact the noises we made so startled the attendants that they rushed up to see if we were really in our right minds. I suspect the noise the three of us made was more noise than had ever disturbed the peaceful quiet of the old temple since the days it was built and this we learned was more than ten thousands years ago. In fact it was so old that it looked a part of the rock upon which it rested.

When we arrived on the roof there was no need to ask for quiet. One look and my two associates' eyes and mouths went wide open. I suspect, had anyone looked at mine, they would have seen the same. I waited for them to speak. Almost in one breath came the exclamation, "Why, we are surely suspended in mid-air." They said the sensation was exactly like that I had experienced in the other temple. They had forgotten for a moment that there was anything under the feet and the sensation was that they were floating in mid-air. One remarked, "I do not wonder that these men can fly after experiencing this."

We were aroused from our reveries by a laugh and all turned to find Emil, Jast, and our friend of the records standing close behind us. One of my associates walked quickly up to them, tried to grasp all of their hands at once, and said, "This is wonderful! We do not wonder you are able to fly after you have been here for a time." They smiled and one said, "You are as free to fly as we. You only need to know that you have the power within to do so, then use the power." We then turned to the outlook. The fog had lowered and was floating in great billowy waves just high enough so that not a foot of land could be seen anywhere and the movement of the banks of fog all around gave the sensation that we were being carried on noiseless wings along with the fog. Standing there looking far out, one lost sense of anything underfoot and it was very difficult to believe that we were not floating in space. As I looked out, it seemed as if my body lost all sense of weight and that I was actually floating above the roof. I had so far forgotten myself that when one of the party spoke, my feet hit the roof with such force that I felt the effects of the jar for several days after.

At breakfast that morning we decided to stay over for three days, as we expected to visit only one other place of interest before going on to the appointed meeting place. Upon reading the messages Emil had brought, we learned that our Chief's party had visited this temple only three days before. After breakfast we went out and found the fog gradually clearing. We watched it until it cleared entirely and the sun came up. We could see the little village nestling close in under the cliff and the valley far below.

Our friends decided to visit the village and we asked if we might go with them. They laughed and said we could but they thought we had better use the basket as we would present a better appearance if we did than if we attempted their mode of travel. So we lowered one by one to the ledge, then down to the little plateau just above the village. No sooner had the last one stepped from the basket than our friends were there. We went down to the village and spent the greater part of the day. It was a quaint old place, typical of those mountain districts with its houses built by digging into the side of the cliff, then closing up the opening with rock walls. There were in all about twenty of these houses. We were told that the houses were built in this manner to keep them from being crushed by the heavy snows in winter. The villagers soon began to gather and Emil talked to them for a few moments. It was arranged that a meeting should be held the following afternoon and couriers were sent out to notify those of the neighborhood who wished to attend.

We were told that John the Baptist had lived at this village and received instruction in the temple and that the temple remained the same as when John received his instruction there. We were shown where the house had been torn down. That afternoon, when we returned to the temple, the weather had cleared so that we could see a wide expanse of country and we were shown the trail that John had used in going to and from the temple and the different villages where he lived. The temple was supposed to have been built and the village established more than six thousand years before John visited there. We were shown the trail we would take when we departed and were told the trail had been in use since the temple was built. About five o'clock that afternoon, our friend of the records said he would leave us for a time. He then shook hands, saying he would see us soon and disappeared.

That evening we saw the most remarkable sunset from the roof of the temple that I have ever witnessed and it has been my good fortune to have seen sunsets in nearly all lands. As evening advanced, a light haze was gathering over a low range of mountains that bordered a wide expanse of table lands which we could look down upon. When the sun reached this rim, we were seemingly so far above it that it appeared as if we were looking directly down upon a sea of molten gold. Then came the afterglow and every mountain peak appeared to be aflame. Those in the distance that were covered with snow seemed to be blanketed with fire and, where glaciers filled the ravines, it appeared as though they were shooting forth great tongues of fire and these flames appeared to meet and melt with the different hues in the heavens. The lakes that dotted the plain below were transformed suddenly into volcanoes belching forth fires which ascended and blended with the colors in the heavens. For one moment it seemed as if we were standing on the brink of a silent inferno; then all blended into one harmony of color and the soft peaceful quiet was beyond description.

We sat on the roof until after twelve that night asking Emil and Jast questions. These questions pertained principally to the people and the history of the country in general. Emil quoted liberally from their records. These records proved that this country was inhabited thousands of years before our history began. Emil went on to say, "While I do not in any way wish to disparage or make light of your history or of those who wrote it, I will say that at the beginning of this history the historians did not go back far enough, but took for granted that Egypt meant what the name implied, outer darkness or the wilderness. It really meant a wilderness of thought. At that time as now, a large portion of the world was in wilderness of thought and they did not go back of it to get the deeper meaning. They accepted what they saw or heard or what appeared on the surface, recorded it, and your history began. It is quite difficult to correlate the two and I would not attempt to say that you must take ours as authentic. I would suggest that you choose for yourselves."

The moon then appeared over the far-off mountains. We sat and watched it round and full until it rose nearly overhead. It was a beautiful sight with an occasional light cloud passing by at an elevation just above us. When these clouds went drifting by it seemed as if the moon and clouds were standing still and we were drifting past them. This went on for an hour when, suddenly, there was a noise as of some object thrown to the roof behind us. We started to our feet and looked around. There stood a middle-aged lady, smiling and asking if she had startled us. Our first impression was that she had jumped from the parapet to the roof but she had only stamped her foot to attract our attention. The stillness had been so intense we had greatly magnified the sound.

Emil stepped forward quickly, greeted her, and introduced us to his sister. She smiled and asked whether she had intruded on our dreams. We then sat down and in a short time the conversation drifted into reminiscences of her experiences. She has three sons and a daughter that had been raised in the work. She replied that the youngest two were always with her. We asked if we might see them. She replied that they could come there that evening; and immediately two figures, a man and a woman, appeared. They greeted their uncle and their mother, then came forward and were introduced to the three of us. The son was a tall, erect, manly fellow, whom we took to be about thirty years of age. The daughter was not tall, rather slight, with very fine features; she was a fine, well-poised girl, whom we judged about twenty years of age. Afterwards, we found that the son was one hundred fifteen and the daughter was one hundred twenty-eight years old. They were all to be present at the meeting the next day and soon went below.

After they had retired we passed complimentary

remarks about the son and daughter. The mother turned to us and said, "Every child born is good and perfect. There are no bad children. It does not matter whether they are conceived in the perfect or immaculate or through the sense or material way. The one conceived in the perfect way will soon recognize his Sonship with the Father, that he is the Christ or Son of God; then he will develop and unfold quickly and he will see only perfection. The one conceived through the sense way may also immediately recognize his Sonship, perceive that the Christ is in him, and may realize his perfection by idealizing the Christ. He gazes upon that ideal, loves and cherishes it until he manifests or brings forth that which he gazes upon, the Christ. He is re-born and is perfect. He has brought forth perfection from within himself, that perfection which was always there. The one held to the ideal and was perfect; the other perceived the ideal and unfolded that ideal, and regained perfection. Thus no child is bad; all are good and from God." Here one of the party suggested that it was bedtime, as it was past twelve o'clock.

CHAPTER XIX

FIVE o'clock the next morning found us all assembled on the roof of the temple. After the regular morning greetings, we gathered around and, as is the usual custom, a selection was read. The selection this morning was from the records of the temple. Jast translated them and we were surprised to find that the translation closely corresponded to the first chapter of St. John in our Bible, and the second reading corresponded to the first chapter of Luke. After the reading, we asked if we might get our Bible and compare the versions. They readily consented and, with the assistance of Jast, we made the comparison and were surprised at the similarity. We had scarcely finished when the breakfast call sounded and all went in. After breakfast we prepared to descend to the village and, for the time, the comparison left our minds.

When we arrived we found quite a number congregated from the near-by country and were told by Jast that they were nearly all shepherds that pastured their flocks in the high mountains in summer, and the time for leaving the lower regions was fast approaching. We were told that such a meeting as would take place that afternoon was always called just before the people departed.

As we walked through the village we met Emil's nephew and he suggested we go for a short walk before lunch. We accepted the invitation readily as we wished to see some of the country around. While we were on this walk, several places were pointed out in the valley as being of special interest. The names, when translated, very closely resembled those of the earlier Bible names, but the real significance of all this did not present itself until we had returned, had lunch, and were seated among those that had assembled.

There were about two hundred in this assembly, when the rest of our friends from the temple appeared. Then Emil's nephew arose and approached two men holding what looked to us like a large book. When this was opened it proved to be a box in the form of a book. He selected a package which consisted of flat leaves like those of a manuscript; then the box was placed on the ground. The package was handed to one of the men. He opened it and handed the first leaf to Emil's nephew. When the reading of each leaf was finished, it was handed to the other man who placed it in the box. The reading proceeded, with Jast as interpreter. It had not gone very far when we saw that it bore a striking resemblance to the Book of St. John, carried out much more in detail. Then followed one similar to that of Luke, then one similar to that of Mark, and the final one was like that of Matthew.

After the reading the people collected in little groups and we, with Jast, sought Emil, for we were curious to know the meaning of it all. We were told that these records were read each year at the meeting and that this place was the center of the country where these scenes were enacted long years ago. We remarked the similarity of these happenings with those chronicled in our Bible and were told that there was no question but that some of the earlier scenes as chronicled in our Bible were taken from these records; but those happenings of a later date, such as the Crucifixion, took place elsewhere, the whole reaching its climax in the Birth and Life of Christ. The foremost thought of it all was the search for the Christ in man and to show those who had wandered away from the ideal that the Christ lived in them as He always had. Emil went on to say it does not matter where the scenes were enacted, it is the underlying spiritual significance which we wish to perpetuate.

We spent the balance of the afternoon and the next day making comparisons and taking notes. Space will not permit the inclusion here of these notes and comparisons but the spiritual meaning will be understood by reading these chapters mentioned above. We found that the father of Emil's nephew who read the records to us was born in the village and was a direct descendant of John and that it was the custom for some member of the family to come to this place at this time and read these records. The temple above us was the one where Zacharias and John both had worshipped.

We found that our friends wished to be on their way, so it was arranged that Jast would stay with us and the others would go on. We finished with the records the next day, then left the temple early the morning after. Although the hour was early, nearly all the villagers were up to bid us "God-speed."

CHAPTER XX

T HE next five days our trail led us through the country that John had traveled. The fifth day brought us to the village where our horses were waiting for us. Here Emil met us and from this time on the traveling was comparatively easy to the village where Emil lived.

As we neared this village we could see that the country was more thickly populated and the roads and trails were far better than any we had traveled. Our way led along the fertile valley and we were following this valley to what happened to be a level plateau. We noticed that the valley was gradually getting narrower as we went on and at last the walls came in so close on each side of the stream that they formed a canyon. About four o'clock of the day we reached the village we came suddenly to a perpendicular bluff over which the stream fell in a drop of about three hundred feet. The road led to a level place at the foot of the cliff, near the falls. We found that there was an opening cut in the sandstone on an angle of forty-five degrees to the plateau above and steps had been hewn in the floor of the upraise so that the ascent was an easy one. Great stone doors had been so arranged that they could be closed into the opening at the foot of the cliff, thus presenting a formidable barrier to an intruding foe. When we reached the plateau above, we found the stairway up the incline was the only means of egress or ingress that the creek afforded. At one time there had been three means of access but the walls that surrounded the village had now been rebuilt in such a way as to bar all possible access. A great many houses in the village were built so that one wall formed a part of the wall that surrounded the village. We noted that, when the houses formed part of the wall, these houses were usually three stories high and there were no openings for windows in the wall until the third story was reached. At every opening a balcony was built large enough for two or three people to stand upon comfortably. These, we judged, were arranged so that a lookout could be kept at all times. We were told the district was once inhabited by a native tribe that isolated themselves from the others until as a tribe they had disappeared, a few having been assimilated by the other tribes.

This was Emil's home and the place where we were to meet the members of our party who had divided into small groups in order to cover more territory. Upon inquiry we found we were the first to arrive and that the others would be in the next day. We were assigned to one of the houses built into the wall of the village. The windows of the third story looked out over the rugged mountainous country to the south. We were made comfortable and were told that supper would be served on the first, or ground floor. We went down and found Emil, his sister, her husband, and the son and daughter that we had met at the temple a few days before, seated at the table.

We had no sooner finished supper than we heard a commotion in the little square which the house faced. One of the villagers came in and announced that our Chief and his party had arrived. They were made comfortable; then we all proceeded to the roof.

The sun had gone down but the afterglow still lingered. The view we looked out upon resembled a large basin at the confluence of a number of streams coming down in deep gorges from the higher mountains. These streams all entered the larger stream before it flowed over the steep wall of rocks into the valley below, thus forming the waterfall. This larger stream emerged from a deep canyon and ran over the level plateau but a few hundred feet before it plunged over the precipice. A number of smaller streams flowed over the perpendicular walls of the canyon cut by the larger stream, forming perpendicular falls and in some cases, roaring torrents. Some fell in sheer drops of one to two hundred feet while others had cut their way into the canyon wall and fell in a succession of cataracts. Far up in the mountains the gulches were filled with glaciers and these glaciers projected like giant fingers from the great snowcap that covered the top of the entire range. The wall to protect the village had been joined to that of the larger gorge where it jutted out upon the level plain, then ran out to the cliff where the water dropped into the valley below. Where this wall joined the wall of the gorge the mountain rose perpendicular for two thousand feet, thus creating a natural barrier as far as the eye could see. We were told that the level plateau extended for sixty miles east and west and in some places was thirty miles north and south; and the only other means of access was at the widest part of the plateau where a trail led over a pass; and this pass was guarded by a wall similar to the one where we were.

While we were talking over the advantages of the location for defense, Emil's sister and her daughter joined us and a little later Emil, his sister's husband and son, came up. We noticed an undercurrent of excitement and were soon told by Emil's sister that they expected a visit from their mother that evening. She said, "We are so happy that we can hardly contain ourselves, for we do love mother so. We love all that have gone on to the higher attainments very dearly, for they are so fine and noble, and helpful, but our own mother is so sweet and adorable, so helpful and loving, we cannot help loving her a thousand times more. Besides, we are of her flesh and blood. We know you will love her as we do." We asked whether she came often. The reply was, "O yes, she always comes when we need her, but she is so taken up with her work that she comes only twice a year of her own accord and this is one of her semi-annual visits. She is to stay a week this time and we are all so happy we scarcely know what to do."

Here the talk drifted to experiences of our associates while we were separated and we were deep in this discussion when, suddenly, stillness came over all and almost before we realized it we were sitting perfectly silent, without a suggestion from anyone. The evening shadows had gathered until the far-off mountain's snowcap looked like a great white monster just ready to loose its icy fingers and reach out over the valley below. From the stillness came a gentle swish like that of a bird alighting and it seemed as though a slight mist were gathering on the eastern parapet. The mist suddenly took form and there stood a woman, wondrously beautiful in face and form, with an intense radiant light about her that we could scarcely look upon. The family started to their feet and advanced rapidly toward her with outstretched arms, exclaiming "Mother," almost as one voice. She stepped lightly down from the parapet to the roof and embraced each as any fond mother would, then was introduced to us. She said, "Oh, you are the dear brothers from far-away America that have come to visit us. I certainly am overjoyed to welcome you to our land. Our hearts go out to all and we feel that if they would only let us, we would just put our arms out and embrace all as I have embraced these I call mine, just now. For we are in reality one family, sons of the one Father-Mother God. Why can we not all meet as brothers?"

We had remarked just before that the evenings were growing chilly, but when this lady appeared the warmth emitted from her presence made the evening seem like that of midsummer. The air seemed laden with the perfume of flowers, a light like that of the full moon seemed to pervade everything, and there was a warmth and glow over all that I cannot describe. Yet there was no hint of display; just that deep, simple, kindly, childlike way.

It was suggested that we go below and the mother with the other ladies led the way to the stairs, with our party following and the men of the household bringing up the rear. Then we noticed that, although we seemed to be walking in the usual way, our feet made no sound upon the roof or the stairs. We were not trying to go quietly; in fact, one of our party said he deliberately tried to make a noise and could not. It did not seem as if our feet came in contact with the roof or stairs. We went into a beautifully furnished room. As soon as we entered and were seated we noticed a warmth and glow and the room was filled with a soft light that none of us could explain.

All maintained a deep silence for a time. The mother asked if we were comfortably located and cared for and if we were enjoying our trip. The talk led to general everyday subjects and she seemed familiar with them all. The talk then led to our home life and the mother gave us the given names of fathers, mothers, sisters and brothers, and we were surprised at the detailed description of each of our lives that she gave without asking us one question. She told us the countries we had visited, the work we had accomplished, and where we had failed. This was not told in a vague way that we would be obliged to piece together but every detail stood out as plainly as if we were living the scenes over again. After our friends bade us goodnight, we could but wonder, when we realized that not one of them was less than one hundred years old and the mother was over seven hundred years and six hundred of that time she had lived on earth with her physical body. Yet all were as buoyant and light-hearted as though they had been twenty, and nothing was assumed. It was as though youthful people were with us. Before they departed that evening we were told there would be quite an assembly in the lodge the next evening and that we were all invited to be present.

CHAPTER XXI

BEFORE noon of the next day all of the parties had arrived. We spent the afternoon in comparing notes and these notes checked to the letter. That evening, after we had finished with our notes, we were invited to go directly to the lodge for dinner. When we arrived we found about three hundred people—men, women, and children—assembled and seated at long banquet tables. They had reserved places for us at one of the end tables so we could look down the whole length of the room. The tables were all covered with beautiful white linen and set with china and silverplate as for a real banquet; yet there was but one dim light burning in the hall.

After we had been seated for perhaps twenty minutes, there was a deep stillness and in a moment a pale light flooded the room. The light grew stronger and stronger until all the room was aglow and everything in the room sparkled as if thousands of incandescent lamps had been cunningly hidden and turned on gradually until all were fully lighted. We were to learn afterwards that there were no electric lights in the village. After the light came on, the stillness lasted for about fifteen minutes, then of a sudden, a mist seemed to gather and there was the same gentle swish like the sound of wings that we had heard the evening before when Emil's mother appeared before us. The mist cleared and standing in the room at different points were Emil's mother and eleven others; nine men and three women.

Words fail to describe the radiant beauty of that scene. When I say that, although they had no wings, they appeared like a troop of angels, I am not exaggerating. They stood for an instant as if transfixed. All bowed their heads and waited. In a moment there came music from unseen voices. I had heard of heavenly voices but I had never experienced them until that night. We were fairly lifted from our seats. Toward the close those that had appeared walked to their seats and we again noticed that, though they made no effort to walk quietly, their feet did not make the slightest noise.

When the twelve were seated in their respective places the same mist appeared again and when it cleared there stood twelve more. This time there were eleven men and one woman and among these was our friend of the records. As they stood there for a moment another song burst forth. When the song was nearly ended the twelve walked to their respective places without the slightest noise.

They were no sooner seated than the haze again filled the room. When it had cleared there were thirteen standing, this time across the far end of the hall, six men and seven women; three men and three women on each side of the woman in the center. The center one appeared to be a beautiful girl in her teens. We had thought every woman that appeared was very beautiful but this one surpassed them all. They stood with bowed heads for a moment and the music again burst forth. This music floated out for a moment then the choir of voices began. We arose to our feet. As the tones rolled on, it seemed as though we could see thousands of mystical forms moving about and singing as with one voice and through it all there was not one sad refrain, not one minor key. All was a joyous, free burst of music that came from the soul and touched the soul, lifting it up and up until we felt as if we were losing all contact with the earth.

As the singing ceased, the thirteen walked to their respective places and were seated. Our eyes were fairly glued on the central figure as she advanced toward our table, with a lady on either side. She was seated at the head of our table. As she sat down, the plates were quietly stacked at her left hand. The lights grew dim for a moment and around each one of the thirty-seven there was that same light that so puzzled us and the most beautiful circle of light just above the head of our honored guest. We were the only ones in that assembly that were greatly moved. Those assembled with us seemed to take it as a matter of course.

After all were seated, the silence was maintained for a time; then every voice in the room burst forth in a glad, free chant led by the thirty-seven that had appeared. When this was finished, the lady at the head of our table arose and held out her hands. On them appeared a small loaf of bread about two inches square and about fourteen inches long. Then each one of the other thirty-six arose, came forward, and received a similar loaf from her hands. They passed around to all the tables and gave to each one a portion of the bread. Our lady passed around and gave each one a portion of her loaf.

As she handed each of us our portion she said, "Know ye not that Christ dwells within you and in all? Know ye not that your body is pure, perfect, young, ever beautiful, divine? Know ye not that God created you an exact image and likeness of Himself and gave you dominion over all things? You, of yourself, are always Christ, the perfect Son of God, the only begotten Son of God, in whom the Father-Mother is well pleased. You are pure, perfect, holy, divine, one with God, all Good, and each and every child has a right to claim this Sonship, this Divinity." When all had been given a portion, she returned to her seat and the loaf was the same length and size as it was when she broke the first portion from it.

After this ceremony was over, the edibles began to arrive. They came in large covered containers. These containers just appeared on the table before the lady as if they were placed there by unseen hands. She lifted the lids, set them aside, and began serving. As served, the plates were passed, first one to the lady on the right, then one to the lady on the left; and they in turn passed them on until all were served generously.

The meal had not progressed far when our Chief asked the lady what she considered the greatest attribute of God. Without a moment's hesitation she answered, "Love." Then she went on to say, "The Tree of Life is located in the midst of the paradise of God, the very depth of our own soul, and the rich, abundant fruit that grows and ripens to the fullest perfection, the most perfect and life-giving, is Love. Love has been defined by those who perceive its true character as the greatest thing in the world. I might add that it is the greatest healing force in the world. Love never fails to meet every demand of the human heart. The Divine Principle of Love may be used to eliminate every sorrow, every infirmity, every harsh condition, and every lack that harasses humanity. With the right understanding and use of the subtle and illimitable influence of love, the world may be healed of its wounds and the sweet mantle of its heavenly compassion may cover all inharmony, all ignorance, and all mistakes of mankind.

"With wings outstretched, Love searches out the arid spots of the human heart, the waste places of life, and with seeming magic touch redeems humanity and transforms the world. Love is God, eternal, limitless, changeless, going beyond all vision into infinitude. The end we can only envision. Love fulfills the law of its own, consummates its perfect work, and reveals the Christ within the soul of man. Love is ever seeking an inlet whereby it may flow forth into the soul of man and pour itself out as all good to him. If it is not disturbed by man's perversity and discordant thinking, God's eternal, changeless current of love flows ever onward, carrying before it, into the great universal sea of forgetfulness, every appearance of inharmony or ugliness which disturbs the peace of man. Love is the perfect fruit of the Spirit; it goes forth, binding up the wounds of humanity, drawing nations into closer harmony, and bringing peace and prosperity to the world. It is the very pulse of the world, the heartbeat of the universe. Humanity must be charged with this current of love from the great Omnipresent Life if it would do the works of Jesus.

"Does life press heavily upon you? Do you need courage and strength to meet the problems that confront you? Are you sick or afraid? If so, lift your heart and pray to Him who leads the way. The imperishable love of God enfolds you. You need not fear. Did He not say, 'Before they call I will answer and while they are yet speaking I will hear'? Approach this throne of grace boldly, not as you have thought of beseeching and groveling attitude, but with the prayer of understanding faith, knowing that the help you stand in need of is already yours. Never doubt. Do more—ask. Claim your birthright as the child of the living God, as Jesus did. Know that in the Invisible, Universal Substance, in which we all live and move and have our being, is every good and perfect thing that man can desire, waiting to be drawn forth by faith into visible form or manifestation. Read in your own great Book what Paul says of love in 1 Corinthians, Chapter 13, using the word, 'love,' instead of charity, as was intended.

"Consider Solomon, when in the night of his experience he allowed his radiant love nature to expand to that universal plane of consciousness where he asked to be of service and not for self. This brought to him wealth untold and added to this was life and honor beyond his power to ask. He recognized the wisdom of Love and Love released its boundless wealth upon him. 'Silver was counted as naught in the days of Solomon.' Even the drinking vessels of this mighty king of love were of pure gold.

"To love is to release God's unlimited storehouse of golden treasure. If we love we cannot help giving, and to give is to gain, and the law of love is fulfilled. Then, by giving, we set in operation the unfailing law of measure for measure. With no thought of receiving, it is impossible to avoid receiving, for the abundance you have given is returned to you in fulfillment of the law, 'Give and it shall be given unto you; good measure, pressed down, shaken together, and running over, shall men give unto your bosom. For with the same measure that you mete, withal, it shall be measured to you again.'

"If we work in the spirit of love, we must have God present in consciousness. To be one with Life, Love, and Wisdom, is to consciously contact. To consciously contact God is to have abundance pressed upon us the same as abundance of food has been pressed upon us tonight. You see there is an abundance for all and none need want in the presence of God's abundance. This thought of abundance must lift the mind far beyond the bounds of limitation. To conceive abundance, one must relinquish all thoughts of things in particular. This concept is so large that it will not permit the thought of detail. To hold it in mind, consciousness must swing far out into the Universal and revel in the joyousness of perfect freedom. This freedom must,

[120]

however, not be taken for license, for we are held responsible for every thought, every act. Our consciousness cannot attain to this freedom in an instant. The breaking of the last vestige of limitation may be accomplished in an instant but the preparation for the glorious event has gone before; the preparation in minutest detail has been accomplished from within, just as every petal of a flower is perfected in every detail within the bud. When the perfection is complete, the bud bursts its sepal shell and the flower comes forth beautiful. Just so man must break the shell of self before he can come forth.

"God's laws are changeless, the same as they have ever been. While they are immutable, they are beneficent, for they are good. When we live in conformity to them, they become the very foundation stones on which we build our health, our happiness, our peace and poise, our success and attainment. If we abide fully in God's law, no evil can befall us. We do not need to be healed. We are every whit whole.

"How well we realize that in the great heart of humanity there is a deep homesickness which never can be satisfied with anything less than a clear consciousness or understanding of God, our Father. We recognize this hunger as hearts cry after God. There is nothing the human soul so longs for as to know God, 'Whom to know aright is life eternal.' We see people ever shifting from one thing to another, hoping they will find satisfaction or rest in some accomplishment or in the possession of some limited, mortal desire. We see them pursuing and gaining these things only to find themselves still unsatisfied. Some fancy they want houses and lands; some, great wealth; and some, great learning. We are privileged to know that man has all these things within himself. Jesus, the Great Master, attempted to have all see

[121]

this. How we do love Him! He stands out so beautifully triumphant because of His attainments. We
love all who have reached the heights or high places
in consciousness that Jesus has. We not only love
them for their attainments but because of what they
really are.

"Jesus never allowed Himself to dwell in the
external after His illumination. He always kept His
thoughts at the central part of His being, which is
the Christ. In Jesus, the Christ or Central Spark
which is God in us all, living in everyone today, was
drawn forth to show itself perfectly ruling the material body or flesh man. It is in this way that He did all
His mighty works, not because He was in some way
different from you. He had no greater power than all
have today. He was not in some way a Son of God
and we only servants of God. He did these works
because this same Divine Spark, which the Father
has implanted in every child born, was fanned into a
brighter flame by His own efforts in holding Himself
in conscious communion with God Himself, the
source of all Life, Love, and Power.

"Jesus was a man the same as all men are today.
He suffered, was tempted and tried, just as you
suffer because of temptation and trials. We know
that during His residence on earth in the visible body
Jesus spent hours of every day alone with God and we
know that, in His early manhood, He went through
just what we have gone through and what you are
going through today. We know that every man must
overcome the mortal, the fleshly desires, the doubts
and fears, until he comes to the perfect consciousness or recognition of the indwelling Presence, this
'Father in me,' to whom Jesus ascribed the credit of
all His mighty works. He had to learn as we had to
learn and as you are learning today. He was obliged
to try over and over again as you are doing. He was

obliged to hold fast as you are obliged to hold fast today, even with clenched fist and set teeth and saying, 'I will succeed, I do know the Christ lives within me.' We recognize that it was the Christ within which made Jesus what He was, and is today, and that the same attainments are for all. In all this we would in no way detract from Jesus for we love Him with a love unspeakable. We know He went through the perfect crucifixion of self that He might lead His people to God; that He might show them the way out of sin, sickness, and trouble, that they might manifest the Father in them; that He might teach all that the same Father lives in all and loves all. None that follow Jesus' life and teaching closely can help but love Him. He is our perfect elder brother.

"But if we sell our birthright, if we disregard or treat with contempt the beneficent laws of God, and by so doing turn our backs on the Father's house and wander into a far country, as did the prodigal son, of what avail is the peace and plenty, the abundance of warmth and cheer that abides within the house? When you are tired of the husks of life, when you are weary and homesick, with faltering steps you may retrace your way home to the Father's house. This may be done over the road of bitter experience or by a joyful letting go of all material things. It does not matter how the understanding and knowledge is gained, you will eventually press on toward the mark of your high calling. With each step you will grow stronger and bolder until you will no longer falter nor hesitate. You will look within you for your illumination; then in your awakened consciousness you will realize that home is here. It is the Divine Omnipresence in which we all live, move, and have our being. We breathe it with every breath. We live it with every heartbeat.

[123]

"Do not think you must come to us. Go into your own home, your church, your house of prayer, alone, anywhere you choose. Jesus the great love Master can help you; all those that have passed and are receiving the highest teachings can help you and are endeavoring to help you where you are now and at all times. How plainly we see Jesus and all the others always ready to help those who call. You need but make the call and they answer before the call is even finished. They stand and walk beside you every moment. What you must do is to raise your consciousness so that you can see and know that you walk beside them; then you will not falter. They are holding out their hands and saying, 'Come unto me and I will give you rest.' This does not mean 'Come after death'; this means 'Come now, just as you are.' Raise your consciousness to our consciousness and behold, you stand where we are tonight, above all mortal limitations, abundantly free.

"Peace, health, love, joy, and prosperity are here. These are the fruits of the Spirit, the gifts of God. If we look unto God, no harm can befall us, no evil can come nigh us. If we look to Him wholly, we are healed of our infirmities, in the transcendent name of the Law, or Jesus.

"God is in the midst of you, child of infinite, immortal Spirit. There is naught to make you tremble or despair, naught to make you fear. From the bosom of the Father you came; the breath of Almighty God created you a living soul. 'Before Abraham was, you were. Beloved now are we Sons of God, joint heirs with Christ.' The same power is in you that is in Jesus. This is called the mantle of the Spirit. With the right concept of this, it is found that there is no decay, no disease, no accident, no death, nothing that can take your life in any way. You can draw this mantle so closely around you that nothing can penetrate it, nothing can touch you. All the destructive agencies or forces ever created by man may be directed at you; yet you will come forth unharmed. If by any chance the outer form should be destroyed, it would immediately return as spiritual in the same form. This is an armor better than any armor plate ever devised by man and you can use it at all times without money and without price. You can stand forth as you are, the child of the living God.

"Jesus recognized this, and He could have saved Himself the Calvary experience. Had He wished to use His power, his enemies could not have touched Him. He saw there was a great spiritual change taking place in His body and saw that, if this was brought about among those He knew and loved, without some outward change, a great many would not recognize the spiritual import but would still cling to the personal. He knew that He had the power to overcome death and He wished to show those that He loved that they had the same power; so He chose the Calvary way, the way they could see; and seeing, they would believe. He also wished to show that He had so perfected His body that, should His enemies take His life (as they looked upon life) and place His body in the tomb and roll a great stone thereon (the last limitation that man could put upon it), still He, the true Self, could roll away the stone and raise His real or spiritual body above all mortal limitations. Jesus could have taken His body and disappeared but He chose to show that, when the spiritual body is developed, no material accident or condition can destroy it, not even the taking of the life by another.

"After the Crucifixion and Ascension His body was so highly developed spiritually that Jesus was obliged to raise the consciousness of those about Him to a plane where they were able to see Him, just as we are obliged to raise the consciousness of nearly all those about us tonight. When the women came to the tomb that morning and found the stone rolled away and the grave clothes lying by, even they did not know Him until He had raised their consciousness to the plane where they could behold Him. Then later, when two were on the road to Emmaus, Jesus drew near and conversed with them, yet they knew Him not until He broke bread with them. At that time their consciousness was raised to the plane where they could behold Him. Just so, when He appeared to others, He even walked and talked with them, yet they did not recognize Him because their consciousness was not functioning on the plane where they could see Him. The moment their consciousness did rise or function on the plane with His, they saw Him. Then some perceived the spiritual import of actuality. They saw the deep meaning underlying it all. They knew. Yet with all this a great many did not believe in Him because they had not yet attained a plane in consciousness where they could see or perceive the underlying spiritual meaning.

"Then the veil of mystery drawn by man's mortal perception was removed. 'And the veil of the temple was rent in twain from the top to the bottom.' The consciousness was attained that death had been overcome; and that not only death, but all man-made mortal limitations could and would be overcome, by coming up over them or raising our consciousness to the plane on which they can no longer be seen and, therefore, do not exist. If this consciousness is loved and cherished it will come forth.

"This was the revelation that came to Jacob as he lay upon the hard stone of materiality. It was revealed to him that that which is gazed upon is

[126]

brought forth and his realization of this released him from his material bondage. It was this which prompted him to put spotted sticks in the cows' drinking water, thus causing them to bring forth spotted offspring.

"We can so definitely put forth our ideal into the formless that it is formed direct from the unformed, that which appears invisible to mortal consciousness. The drinking water of the cows but typifies the mirror through which the image held in mind is reflected to the soul, the innermost, and then conceived and brought forth. It is the same with the friends assembled here tonight; only a few of the earnest ones perceive and they go on, unfold, and do the real work of God. Others make a good beginning but it soon requires too much exertion to surmount the first wall of materiality. They find it much easier to drift with the tide and they drop out. We have all lived in the visible, mortal plane on this earth. In fact, we have never left the earth. We are now invisible only to those that are in mortal consciousness. To those that are on a higher plane of consciousness we are always visible.

"Every seed idea placed in the soul becomes a conception and is given thought-form in mind, later to be experienced in physical form. Ideas of perfection produce perfection. The reverse is equally true. Just as the sun and the earth produce with equal willingness the mighty tree or the frailest flower, when their respective seeds are planted, so Spirit and Soul respond to man and that which he desires or that for which he has asked, believing, he receives.

"Those that have passed from the visible through death are manifesting on the same psychic plane as when they left the body, for the mortal mind functions on the psychic plane. This is the cause of the great psychic realm which lies between the material, or visible, and the true spiritual, and through which all aspiring to the true spiritual must force their way before the spiritual is perceived. In order to perceive the spiritual, we must forge through the psychic directly to God. Death releases the soul only to the psychic plane and it manifests on the same spiritual plane it was in when the soul was released from the body. The one so passing has not perceived that there is but one Spirit, one Mind, one Body and that all came forth from this One and must return to it. The Spirit sent forth from this One and given a perfect body is as much a part of the One Spirit as our arm is a part of our whole body; and is never separated from it any more than any member of our body is a separate part, but is one with the whole body and must be fitly joined with it to make up the whole. So must all spirit or expression be fitly joined together to be complete and perfect.

"'They shall all be gathered together in one place,' means that we shall be conscious that we are one expression of the Divinity and all from the same source, God. This is the atonement, the at-one-ment, knowing we are all created in the image and likeness of God, exactly like Him, an image through which He may and can express the ideal He has conceived for us.

"To be willing that God shall express perfectly through us the highest ideal He has conceived is the meaning of, 'Not my will, but Thine, O God, be done.' None can rise above mortal thoughts without doing the will of God whether he does it consciously or unconsciously."

Here the talk dropped for a moment and one of our party asked about the Relativity of Matter. She went on to say, "The real world is Substance, the Relativity of Substance. Let us consider for a moment the five kingdoms: the mineral, the vegetable, the animal, the man, and the God kingdoms. We will begin at the mineral, the lowest. We find every particle of the mineral kingdom expressing the one life, the life of God. The disintegration or division of the particles of the mineral, combined with elements of air and water, has formed soil, every particle still retaining the original life, the life of God. This gives place to the vegetable kingdom, the next higher expression of God to come forth. Then the vegetable, every part of which contains this one life, has taken up a part of this life from the mineral, has increased and multiplied it, and is expressing it one step higher toward the God kingdom. This gives place to the animal, the next higher expression of God. Then the animal, every part of which contains the one life, has taken up a part of this life from the vegetable, has increased and multiplied it, and is expressing one step higher toward the God kingdom. This gives place to the man kingdom, the next higher expression of God. Then the man kingdom, every part of which contains the one life, has taken up a part of this one life from the animal kingdom and, in expressing it one step higher, gives place to the God kingdom, the highest expression through man. When man has attained this kingdom, he recognizes that all have come forth from the one Source, that all contain the one life, the life of God, and he has gained the mastery over all material things. But we need not pause here, for all is progression. When he arrives here he will find there are new worlds still to conquer. Now we come to the place where we recognize that all space or magnitude contains the one life, the life of God, that all is from the one Source and Substance. Then all substance becomes relative or related, does it not?"

Here the talk ended, the dinner was finished, and

the room was cleared of tables and chairs. There followed a time of frolic and fun, including dance and song with the music furnished by the invisible choir, and all enjoyed a good time together. The evening finally ended in music and song; the invisible choir became visible, walked among those assembled, and at times floated just above their heads. The final ending was one outburst of music, song, and laughter, with all participating. Taken altogether, it was the most impressive scene that we ever witnessed.

We were told that if we would become quiet, we could hear the music at all times, but it is only on an occasion like this that the chorus accompanies the music. We tried this a number of times afterward and found that we could hear the music. It was always low and beautifully sweet but it never had the glad free ring of that one evening unless there were a number of the Masters congregated. We were told that this music is what has been called the angel choir. They call it "the symphony of souls in accord."

We stopped in this village three days and during that time saw a great deal of our friends. The evening of the third day they bade us goodbye and, saying they would meet us at our winter quarters, disappeared.

CHAPTER XXII

T HE next morning we left the village with only Emil and Jast accompanying us, our objective being the village we had decided upon for our winter quarters. The winters in this part of the country are quite severe and we felt that we wished to make certain of comfortable quarters before the cold spell set in. In this as in a great many other matters our fears were not well grounded for when we arrived we found comfortable quarters all ready for us.

Our trail from the village led across the plateau, then up a long winding canyon to the divide where the second fortified village that guarded the plateau we had crossed was located. The canyon walls were from two hundred to five hundred feet perpendicular and joined the mountains which rose to an elevation of two thousand feet above the crest where the trail crossed the divide. At the top of the divide two great rock ridges jutted up on either side of a level space about five acres in extent. These two ridges were about six hundred feet apart. A wall forty feet high had been built across the open space, thus connecting the two ridges of rock and forming an effectual barrier. This wall was sixty feet wide at the bottom and thirty feet wide at the top and was so constructed that the top formed a runway over which huge rocks could be rolled, then dropped to the ground on the outer side of the wall where the ground sloped sharply and connected with a steep declivity, down which the trail passed on the way to the other side of the divide.

There were chutes arranged along the wall at intervals of one hundred feet so that the rocks would gain headway enough to clear the base of the wall before they struck the ground. When they did strike they would roll down the slope, then over the declivity and on down the canyon for about four miles before they would stop, if they did not fly into pieces from their own momentum. In all, this formed an effectual defense, as the canyon was not over fifty feet wide at any place in the four miles, and it was steep enough to give great momentum to the rolling rocks. There were also two places on each side of the canyon where rocks could be loosened and would roll down. These places were connected by trails cut along the mountain side from each end of the wall. There were a number of rocks, each about twelve feet through, placed along the top of the wall ready for an emergency. We were told that it had not been found necessary to use any of them, as there was but one tribe that had ever attempted to gain access to the village uninvited, and this tribe had been all but annihilated by rocks released from the four stations in the canyon walls. The first rocks released in their downward course had released others until an avalanche swept down the valley, carrying all before it. We were told the rocks on top of the wall had rested where they were for over two thousand years, as there had not been a war in that country during that time.

We found that the six houses comprising the village were built into the wall, three stories high, with the roofs level with the top of the wall. Access to it was thus gained by stairways leading up through each story to the roof of each house. Openings for windows were left in the wall at the third story. These windows overlooked the canyon below. The trail could be seen from these windows and the top of the wall, as it wound around the mountain side, miles away.

We were made comfortable for the night in the third story of one of these houses and, after an early dinner, we went to the roof to see the sunset. We had been there but a few moments when a man apparently fifty years of age came up the stairs to the roof. After being introduced by Jast he joined in the conversation. We soon found he lived in the village we had selected for our winter quarters and was on his way there. We supposed he was traveling as we were and invited him to join our party. He thanked us and said he was able to make the distance much more quickly than we could, that he had stopped in the village to see a relative, and would be home that evening. The conversation then turned to the temple the three of us had visited with Emil and Jast. This man spoke quietly and said, "I saw you sitting on the parapet of the temple that night." Then he went on and gave the dream or vision just as it came to me and as it has been set forth in this book. This came as a surprise to me and my associates as I had not mentioned the occurrence to them. This man was a perfect stranger to us, yet he recounted the dream as vividly as it had appeared to me.

Then he went on to say, "You were shown just what we are shown, that man comes forth in unity just as long as he has consciously realized this and used the power and dominion rightly; but the moment he, in his mortal self, conceived dual powers, he began to see dual, he misused this power, and brought forth duality, for man is a free will agent and brings forth that which he gazes upon. Then diversity and wide separation resulted and this has followed him all over the earth. But a change is coming. Diversity has about reached its limit and mankind is recognizing that all came forth from the

[133]

one Source. Recognizing this, men are now coming closer and closer together. Man is beginning to realize that every other man is his brother instead of his enemy. When man does fully realize this, he will see that just as all came from the one Source, all must return to that Source or become as brothers in reality. Then he will be in heaven and will recognize that heaven means the inner peace and harmony created by man right here on earth. He will then see that he makes his heaven or hell just as he chooses. This heaven has been conceived rightly but misplaced geographically. He will know that God dwells within him and not only within him but in everything about him, every rock, every tree, every plant, every flower, and every created thing; that God is in the very air he breathes, the water he drinks, the money he spends; that God is the substance of all things. When he breathes, he breathes God as much as he does air; when he partakes of food, he partakes of God as much as he does of food.

"It is not our wish to form new cults, or sects. We feel that the churches that are established today are sufficient and they are the logical centers to reach out and help the people to the realization of God, through the Christ in all. Those associated with the churches must realize that the church but typifies the one thing, the Christ Consciousness in all mankind. If they realize this, where can the diversity lie but in the concept of man's mortal mind and not in the church? Wherein then is one church or society different from another? The diversity thought to exist today must be wholly in man's mortal mind. See what this diversity has led to, the great wars, the intense hate engendered between nations and families and even individuals, and all because one church organization or another has thought that its creed or doctrine was better than that of another. Yet all in reality are the same for they all lead to the same place. It would not be possible for each to have a heaven of its own; for if it did, when a fellow-man finished with his particular brand of church organization and was ready to receive his reward, he would be obliged to spend the remainder of his existence looking through the maze of heavens for the particular one he is destined for. The church organizations and those associated with them are coming closer each day and the time will come when they will be united as one. When all are as one, there will be no need of organization.

"Yet the fault does not lie wholly with church organizations. Few people have awakened to the realization of what life really holds for them. We find the greater majority drifting through life, dissatisfied, dazed, crushed, or uncertain. Each must learn to lay hold of life and begin to express, from his own life center, with purposeful, definite action, the gifts that God has given him. Each must unfold his own life. It is not possible for one to live for another. No one can express your life for you and none can say how you must express your own life. 'As the Father hath life in Himself, so hath He given unto the Son to have life in Himself.' A soul cannot realize this and just drift, for the whole purpose of life reveals itself in the privilege and opportunity of expressing the God self within. That man is and shall be the divine image and likeness of Himself is God's purpose for man. To express that which God has conceived for him should be man's great purpose in life. When Jesus was on the mountain top and His disciples came to Him, see what words of wisdom He spoke unto them. His consciousness was awakened to this realization and He had become established in this high resolve, that man can unfold in the fullness of power only when he has a true ideal, a real purpose in life. A seed can begin to grow only when it is firmly fixed in the ground. The God power within can bring forth a true desire only when it is firmly fixed in the soul of man. We must all know, as Jesus did, that the first spiritual impulse toward expression is the definite desire to express.

"Jesus said, 'Blessed be the poor in spirit,' realizing that any limitation in life that can create a desire in the individual to rise superior to the limitation and free himself from it is good. He realized that need is the prophecy of fulfillment. He looked upon every need as soil prepared for a seed. If the seed were planted, then allowed to grow and come forth, it would fill the need. Need or desire, in the unfoldment of life, is misunderstood. That it must be crushed out of the heart is taught by some great teachers. Jesus said, 'Woe unto you who are satisfied.' If you are satisfied, you are at a standstill. In order to contact life fully, we must seek each moment to express life fully. Desire for this is the urge toward it. Weary of crawling in the dust of the earth, man yearns to fly, and this longing invites him to find the manifestation of law that will enable him to rise above his present limitations. Finding it, he is able to go where he will, without thought of time or distance. It has been said that man proposes and God disposes. The reverse is true, for God proposes and man disposes; if man is so disposed, he can do all that God does. Cannot the Son do what the Father has done?

"The failure of outer things to satisfy leads the soul to seek the power within. Then the individual may discover that I AM, he may know that within him lies all power to satisfy the soul, to fulfill its every need and desire. This knowledge may not come until the individual is driven by the buffetings of the world to seek this inner plane of peace and calm. When he knows I AM is the fulfillment of his desire, the desire is filled. To look outside the God self for the fulfillment of his desire is folly. To unfold, the self must do the unfolding.

"Then what a realization, what an awakening to know the I AM; to know that within is the power, substance, and intelligence from which all forms take form; and to know that the moment a definite and true idea of desire can be intelligently formed, the power, intelligence, and substance of spirit must flow to it and bring it forth. Are these not treasures in heaven that we have not beheld? Here, in the un-formed, lie boundless treasures hid within ourselves. How clear this is to the one that has found the pearl. Then think, 'Seek ye first the Kingdom of God and His righteousness (right-use-ness) and all these things shall be added unto you.' The reason they are added is that they are made out of the very essence of Spirit. The consciousness must first find the Spirit before it can form the desired thing.

" The awakened one perceives the creative princi-ple within; then he sees and his realization is his life opportunity. He has a vision or becomes aware of his possibilities or the possibilities that lie before him. With the knowledge that the creative power lies within, he recalls his heart's desire; this becomes an ideal, or mold, that draws forth power and substance to fill the mold. I SEE is the soul's conception; it is the Promised Land, the dream come true, toward which the soul may look in faith. Although it may not yet be consciously possessed, it must come forth into visible form as he fulfills the law. A wilderness of experiences may have to be met and overcome. This but makes the soul worthy of atonement. Understanding the vision as a Land of Promise, an ideal that is to be realized or to become real, the soul now sees only the good, the object of its desire. Here there must be no doubt, no wavering, no hesitation, for this would be fatal. One must be true to the vision and press on. This vision is typical and as necessary as the plans and specifications of a building. One must be as true to the vision as the builder is true to the plans and specifications the architect has furnished. All but the truth must be eliminated.

"All great souls are true to their vision. Everything brought forth was first a vision, a seed idea planted in the soul, then allowed to expand and come forth. These souls never allow the unbelief of others to influence them. They are willing to sacrifice for their vision, they are true to it, they believe in it, and it is to them as they believe. Jesus remained true and steadfast to His vision. He adhered to His plan, even when those nearest and dearest to Him were unbelieving and untrue. It was unto Him as He believed and it is so unto all.

"When the individual starts for the Promised Land, the land of darkness must be forsaken, forgotten. He must leave the darkness and start toward the light. It is impossible to go and stay at the same time. The old must be forsaken, the new adhered to. He must forget the things he does not wish to remember and remember only the things he wishes to retain. One is as essential as the other. The vision only must be remembered if he wishes it fulfilled. He must remember by holding in mind the vision he wishes to reproduce. He must disremember or refuse to remember the thing he does not wish to reproduce. Every idea, thought, word, or act must be true to the vision in order to bring it forth. This is true concentration, the concentration of devotion, the centering of the forces upon the essential. This is loving the ideal. It is only through love that an ideal can be given expression. Love makes the ideal become the real.

"If at first he fails, he must be determined and press on. This is the exercise of the will, the cry of self-confidence, the expression of faith directing the power toward the ideal. This ideal could never be attained without this conscious direction of power, this exercise of the will; and yet it would be fatal to the ideal if the will, too, were not ideal. The will must possess the same quality as the ideal to serve. If the will does not possess the desire to serve, the power the will wishes to direct cannot be released from the soul. *The will to be served turns the life current against self. The will to serve keeps the life current flowing through self and keeps the self in radiation.* To serve gives purpose to vision; it releases love in life. How can love be expressed unless it flows through the one expressing life? If it flows through the consciousness, the whole organism responds; it thrills every cell with the love it expresses. Then the body becomes harmonized; the soul becomes radiant; the mind becomes enlightened; the thought becomes keen, brilliant, alive, definite; the word becomes positive, true, constructive; the flesh is renewed, purified and quickened; affairs are adjusted and all things assume their true position. The I AM is expressed through the *me* and the *me* is no longer allowed to suppress the I AM. If the body is not obedient to Spirit, how can it express the Spirit? The conscious mind must seek and want the Spirit in order to learn the power of the Spirit. In this way the individual learns to know that Spirit is the fulfillment of the need. In no way can it be given higher expression than when it is allowed to fill the need of others. It is the flowing forth to others that opens the storehouse of Spirit. It is the 'I will to serve' that opens the unlimited storehouse of God to all and brings its realization to the soul.

"The soul has returned to the Father's house as

soon as it has willed to serve. The prodigal who is serving becomes the feasted son; the hireling feeding on the husks becomes the prince of a royal household, the household of his own possibilities. He knows the love of God and understands and appropriates his Father's gift. None but a son can receive this gift. No servant, no hireling can enter into the joy of the son's inheritance. The servant is always seeking to attain; the son has already inherited all that the Father has. When we know that we belong to the Father's household and that we are heir to all that the Father has, then we can begin to live as the Father wishes us to live. 'Behold now are we Sons of God.' The Son consciousness causes the fulfillment; the servant consciousness causes the lack. We will find every desire of the heart fulfilled by the Father as soon as we act the part of the Son in thought, word, and deed. We will find that the Sons of God are free."

Here the speaker arose, bade us goodnight and, with the remark that he hoped to see us when we arrived at winter quarters, departed.

CHAPTER XXIII

W E LEFT the village the next morning. For three days the trail led through a rough mountainous country so sparsely populated that we were obliged to pitch our tents each night. No provisions had been taken along for this trip, yet when food was needed it was there. No sooner were the arrangements made for a meal than an abundance of food was right at hand to be partaken of; and at no time did we see it all consumed; there was always a little left.

The evening of the third day we reached the head of a wide valley, through which valley we were to travel to reach the village of our destination. From this time on our road led through a fertile, well populated valley. We had selected this village as our winter quarters for the reason that it was located in the very heart of the country we were visiting and we felt that it would give us the opportunity we desired to come in daily contact with the people for a longer period of time. A great many of the people we had met in the different places we had already visited lived in this village and they had all extended cordial invitations to visit them. We felt that, by staying in this village for the winter, we would have ample opportunity to observe their daily life more closely.

We reached this village November 20th and made a number of short trips from there until the snow came on and travel was made difficult. We were housed in very comfortable quarters, the people were very kind, and we prepared to enter into the life of the village. All the homes were thrown open to us and we were told that the latchstrings were always out and that they considered all men brothers.

At this time we were invited to share the home of one of the remarkable women that lived in this village, whom we had met before. We felt that we were comfortable and that it was not necessary to trouble her. She insisted that it would be no trouble; so we moved in, bag and baggage, and made her home our home during the remainder of our stay. I shall never forget the first time we met her. It was in a small town near the border. When she was introduced we thought she was not a day over eighteen and we all thought her beautiful. What was our surprise when we were told she was over four hundred years old and one of the most loved of teachers. Her whole life was spent in the work. When we first met her we had been thrown in daily contact with her for nearly two weeks but her true self did not show forth until we saw her in her own home. After living in her home and being in daily contact with her, we could readily see why the people loved her as they did. It was impossible for anyone to do otherwise than love and respect her. We lived at this lady's home and ate at her table from the last of December until the following April. We had ample opportunity to observe her home life and the home life of a number of others in this village and we found their lives ideal. The more we saw all these people the more we loved and respected them. We had ample opportunity to corroborate all that they told us regarding their ages, by records that could not be contradicted, any more than our records can be contradicted.

CHAPTER XXIV

TIME went on until the last of December and the year was drawing to a close. We had noticed that a number of persons were congregating for the one ceremonial event that the Masters participate in practically alone. Each day we were introduced to strangers. All spoke English and we began to feel that we were a part of the village life. One day we were told that the event would take place on New Year's Eve and we were invited to be present. We were also told that, while this event was not for outsiders, it was in no way a secret meeting, that none of their meetings were private. The assembly was for those who had commenced the work, had taken it up in earnest, and had gone far enough to realize that they wanted to live the life; those who had accepted the higher consciousness and realized what this meant in their lives. It was called by some the "Feast of the Passover." These gatherings were usually held at some stated location at this time of year and this place had been chosen for the occasion this year.

The morning of the day appointed for the assembly dawned bright and clear, with the mercury well below zero. It found us all eager for we felt that this evening would add to the many interesting experiences of the trip. We arrived at the appointed place at eight o'clock that evening and found about two hundred assembled. The room was lighted in the same way as the one mentioned before and was very beautiful. We were told that the beautiful young lady who once before had been our hostess would have charge of the services. A few moments after we were seated she entered the room and we all marveled at her youth and beauty. She wore a beautiful white gown but there was no attempt at display.

She stepped quietly to the small platform and began her address. "We are gathered here this evening with the desire to enter into the fuller meaning of passing from a lower to a higher consciousness and we welcome those of you who are prepared for this. At first you followed us, led by your interest in the things you have seen us accomplish, which you at first looked upon with awe and wonder, thinking of them as marvelous. We know you have at this time learned to look upon these things as the everyday occurrences of a life lived as it should be lived, a natural everyday life that God would have us live at all times. By this time you are satisfied that we have not performed any marvels. You realize the true spiritual meaning of what you are doing. The consciousness that functions from the true spiritual plane always interprets all forms in terms of the ideal underlying them; then the great inner meaning is revealed and there is no mystery, consequently no marvel, no miracle. This passing over from a lower to a higher consciousness means putting away the material, where all is discord and inharmony, and taking up and accepting the Christ Consciousness, in which all is beauty, harmony, and perfection. This is the natural way of living, the way God sees us living, and the way so beautifully exemplified by Jesus here on earth. The other is the unnatural, the self way, the hard way. When we realize it, it is so easy, so natural to live the Christ way. Then we come into the Christ Consciousness.

"We have tables spread. This is the only occasion on which we congregate for a feast. It is not a feast such as those in mortal consciousness might think. It is a feast of realization and accomplishment, symbolizing the passing from the mortal to the Christ Consciousness, and so greatly misunderstood throughout the world today. We believe that all of God's children will sit down to such a feast some day with the true realization of its meaning.

"We shall have with us, tonight, a few of those that have so perfected their bodies that they are able to take them into all the Celestial Realms and there receive the highest teachings. They have all lived a certain time here in visible form, then passed on and taken their bodies with them, to a place in consciousness where they are not visible to mortal eyes; and we must raise our consciousness to the Christ Consciousness to converse with them. But those that have so perfected the body that they can take it to this Celestial Realm can return to us and go away at will. They are able to come and instruct all who are receptive to their teaching and appear and disappear at will. It is these that come and teach us when we are ready to receive instruction, sometimes intuitively and at time by personal contact. There will be five of these to break bread with us tonight. Among the five is one especially beloved by us, as she is the mother of one of us and has dwelt among us. (This proved to be Emil's mother.) We will now gather around the tables."

The lights were dimmed for a moment and all sat perfectly quiet with bowed heads. Then the lights came on and the five stood in the room, three men and two women. They were all dressed in white and were radiantly beautiful, with a soft glow of light about each one of them. They walked quietly forward and each took a place left vacant at the head of each table. Emil's mother took the place at the head of our table, with our Chief at her right and Emil at her left. After the five were seated, the edibles began to arrive. It was a simple meal of vegetables, bread, fruit and nuts, but very palatable. The talks that followed were chiefly instructions to those who had assembled for the occasion. They were given in the native tongue and were translated by Jast. I will not include these talks, as the greater part has already been given.

Emil's mother, the last speaker, used perfect English and her voice was clear and concise. These were her words: "We use forces every day that man in the mortal concept laughs at. We who are privileged to see and use these are doing all that we can to have men see and know what they are keeping out of their lives by the thoughts they are holding of the perfect things that are right at hand ready and waiting to be taken hold of. As soon as these forces are taken hold of or appropriated by man, they will be far more real and living than those things that man clings to so desperately in the mortal — clings to because they can be seen, felt, and handled or contacted through the limited mortal senses. You will note that all our comforts in this room and those you are occupying, such as light and heat and even the things you have eaten, are prepared by one of these forces. You may call it light rays or what you will. We see it as a great universal power or force, which, when contacted by man, will work for him far more effectually than steam, electricity, gasoline, or coal; yet we call it one of the least of the forces or powers.

"This force will not only furnish all the power needed by man but it will also furnish heat for all his needs, at all times and in all places, without the consumption of one pound of fuel of any kind. This force is perfectly noiseless; and if man will contact and use it, it will stop a great deal of the noise and confusion that now seems unavoidable. This power is right at hand all about you, waiting for man to contact and use it. When he does contact and use this force, it will be far simpler than steam or electricity. As man is able to do this, he will see that all modes of power and locomotion that he has devised are but makeshifts that he has brought forth in his own mortal concept. He has thought that he, himself, has brought them forth; and he has in this way brought forth only that which he could contact with the mortal senses. He has brought forth imperfect things; whereas if man would see that all is of God and from God expressing through him, all things that he brings forth would be perfect. Man, having free will, has chosen the hard way; and instead of realizing his Sonship with God and using all that God has, he will go on in the hard way until he is driven to realize that there must be, and really is, a better way. He will eventually know that God's way is the only way. Then he will express the perfection that God sees him expressing right now.

"Do you not see how you must be centered in the Father within you, drawing the whole of your good from Him; and how every force of your nature is to operate from the divine self? In the beginning of all expression is God, the Father, within; else God could not be expressed or brought forth."

Here one of our party asked what power or force our thoughts and words had upon our lives. She held out her hand and in a moment a small object was lying in it. She said, "Let me drop this pebble into this bowl of water. You see that the vibrations caused by the pebble's coming in contact with the water radiate from that center in ever-widening circles until they reach the rim of the bowl, or outer edge of the water; where, to the eye, they seem to lose their force and stop. What really happens is this. As soon as the vibrations have reached the limits of the water, they start on their return journey back to the place where the pebble entered the water; and they do not tarry until they reach that center. This exactly represents every thought or word we think or speak. The thought or word sets in motion certain vibrations that go out and on, in ever-widening circles, until they compass the universe. Then they return as they went forth, to the one that sent them out. Every thought or word we think or speak, be it good or bad, returns to us as certainly as we send it forth. This returning is the Day of Judgment spoken of in your Bible. 'Every day will be a day of judgment thereof.' The judgment will be good or evil, just as the word or thought sent out is good or evil. Every idea (thought or word) becomes a seed; this seed idea is sent out, planted in the soul (held in mind), becomes a conception later to be brought forth or expressed in physical form. Thoughts or ideas of perfection bring forth perfection; thoughts or ideas of imperfection bring forth imperfection.

"The sun and earth combined will produce, with equal willingness, the mighty banyan or the smallest flower if the seed is planted. It is in this way that the Soul and Spirit respond to the call of man; and that for which he asks by word or thought, he receives. The only thing that has separated man from heaven is a mist of material thought that man has created around heaven; and this has given rise to the mysteriousness that surrounds all things divine. This veil of mystery is gradually being pulled aside and it is found that there is no mystery. Those establishing their different church organizations have found it expedient to surround the things of God with mystery, thinking to get a closer hold upon the people. But all are now finding that the deep things of God are the real, simple things of life. If not, of what avail are they? All are perceiving that the church but typifies the Christ Consciousness in man, the God center of humanity. They are perceiving the ideal instead of worshiping the idol which has been built by mortal thought. Look at the vast number of heterodox organizations springing up on every hand. Though widely diversified now, they are bound to lead to the one. Has not this one thing come forth to bring the churches to the true realization?

"We who have so perfected our bodies that we are able to take them where we will are privileged to see and be in what is called the Celestial Realm. This realm is known to a great many as the Seventh Heaven. This realm is thought to be the very mystery of mysteries. This again is where man in mortal thought has erred. There is no mystery; we have only reached a place in consciousness where we are able to receive the highest teachings, the place where Jesus is today. It is a place in consciousness where we know that by putting off mortality, we are able to take on immortality; where we know that man is immortal, sinless, deathless, unchangeable, eternal, just as God is and as God sees man. A place where we know the real meaning of the Transfiguration; where we are able to commune with God and see Him face to face. A place where we know that all can come, and receive, and be as we are. We know that, before long, the consciousness of all will be raised to the plane where we can talk with them face to face and see eye to eye. Our withdrawal from their sight is but the raising of our consciousness above that of the mortal and by this we become invisible only to those in mortal consciousness.

"We have to look upon three events. One that happened long ago, the one that typifies to you the birth of the Christ Consciousness in man, the birth of the Babe Jesus. Then the one we can see coming when your great nation accepts and realizes the Christ Consciousness. Then we love to turn to the third and last, the greatest of all splendors, the second and last coming of the Christ, when all know and accept the Christ within, and live and unfold in this consciousness and grow as the lilies grow. This is the Atonement (At-one-ment)."

As she finished, the invisible choir began to sing. The room was at first filled with music which ended in a solemn dirge. Then there was silence for a moment and the choir again burst forth with one glad riot of music, with each measure ending in a boom like the stroke of a great bell. This continued until twelve had been sounded and we suddenly realized that it was twelve o'clock and the New Year was here.

Thus ended our first year with these wonderful people.

ADDENDUM

IN PRESENTING these notes of experiences with the Masters, I wish to emphasize my personal belief in the powers of these Masters and in their demonstration of a great Law—a Law that must carry a profound message to the whole human race. They proved conclusively that there is a Law that transcends death and that all humanity in its evolution is slowly moving forward to understand and use it. The Masters say this Law will be brought forth in America, will be given to the world, and then all may know the way to Eternal Life. This, they acclaim, is the unfoldment of the New Age.

None of the manifestations referred to in these notes were the materialization of the ordinary seance—far from it. It was the higher expression making the body visible and invisible at will—a glorifying and spiritualizing of the flesh. There is a God Law and human beings will soon inherit it, become illumed, and use the body with understanding in full Masterhood.

There is no question but these people have brought the Light through the long ages and they prove by their daily life and works that this Light does exist just as it did thousands of years ago.

B.T.S.

PUBLISHER'S NOTE: *In addition to Volume One, we have published Volumes Two, Three, Four and Five, in which are continued the accounts of Mr. Spalding's experiences.*